ENDORSEME[

I have known Tracy Eckert for many years and I can attest to the fact that there is one burning passion that drives her—zeal for God's house. In the same year that we started 24/7 prayer in Kansas City, God released a download from heaven to Tracy concerning His house and the call to build it, and she has been obedient to the heavenly vision. She has stewarded this message for twenty years, teaching, discipling, building, and creating a place for God to be the focus. There are so many great books out there on people's encounters and revelations; however, I honestly have come to a place that unless the revelation is "fleshed out" in our lives and ministries over decades, then it will miss its intended purpose. Tracy's book, *God's End-Time Temple,* is one of the rare books that is so desperately needed in this hour because it contains a new paradigm of how we do church. Tracy is a prophet and teacher, but most importantly a mother who has invested her life into seeing this message impact this generation, and I wholeheartedly endorse her and this book and pray that God releases it to the four corners of the earth.

COREY RUSSELL
Author and International Prayer Minister

Tracy Eckert's book, *God's End-Time Temple,* is more than a book—it is a high-level prophetic infusion. The revelatory insights and impartation in this book are beyond valuable for those who are hungry to live as "kings and priests" before God in these days. Thank you, Tracy, for sharing your journey, your prophetic visions, and your sound biblical teaching. I love this book!

Dr. Patricia King

Author, Television Host/Producer, Minister

Tracy Eckert does a great job of prophetically writing God's plan to make His vision plain so we, the final generation before Christ's return, can run with God's mandate of rebuilding today's temple. Tracy brings the reader through a historical journey to experience an up-to-date divine appointment with her as she so skillfully describes her modern-day spiritual adventures written in her revelatory book, *God's End-Time Temple.* She explains how Zerubbabel, the grandson of Jehoiachin and captive king of Judah, was the prime builder of the second temple reestablishing the Jewish sacrificial system during the time of the return from the Babylon exile. A direct descendant of David, Zerubbabel was the head of the tribe of Judah who led the first group of captives back to Jerusalem. King Cyrus gave Zerubbabel and the high priest Jeshua his blessing to return the gold and silver vessels that Nebuchadnezzar had previously removed from the temple. For more than twenty long years, Zerubbabel worked with prophets Haggai and Zechariah, priests, and kings to rebuild and dedicate the second temple in 516 BC on the old site, seventy years after the Babylonians destroyed the first temple in 586 BC.

God's modern-day plan is to awaken an apostolic reformation that fully restores the authority of heaven to govern on earth through the internal identity of His bride, the Church. We are the end-time, capstone, "greater works" generation living out the plumb line directives issued by the word of the Lord to Zerubbabel, *"'Not by might nor by power, but by My Spirit,' says the Lord of hosts."*

Dr. Barbie L. Breathitt
President, Breath of the Spirit Ministries, Inc.

When I first met Tracy, I knew that I had found someone who would not only be a lifelong friend and partner in ministry, but more importantly, I knew that I had stepped into a covenant connection with one who had walked faithfully before the Lord as a prophetic pioneer. Tracy's life, much like the lives of many prophetic pioneers before her, has in many ways taken on the appearance of a modern-day parable with remarkable signs and reoccurring wonders. With these signs and through these wonders, Tracy has prophetically unveiled profound Kingdom keys that have resulted in the call to rebuild God's temple.

As I was reading through the revelations and prophetic words contained in this book, I was reminded how the Lord had shown me years ago that Tracy's posture had been like that of one of David's mighty men, Eleazar, in Second Samuel 23. Eleazar was one of the three mighty men with David when they defied the Philistines. It was said of Eleazar that he had arose and attacked the Philistines until his hand was weary, and his hand stuck to the sword. The Lord brought about a great victory that day; and the people returned after him only to plunder.

Much like Eleazar, Tracy has faithfully held onto the sword of God's promised word to her beyond the magnitude of her own might and past the place of her own power to enter into a far greater place of strength, victory, and vindication that can only come by the Spirit of God Himself. As a faithful prophetic pioneer, Tracy has graciously paved the way for us to enter into that place as well.

Much of the understanding that has accompanied the apostolic wisdom found in this book was divinely concealed in the life and leadership of Zerubbabel and the steps he took to rebuild the temple of his day. With present revelation and practical understanding of past prophetic promises, Tracy pieces together what has become a precise prophetic picture and model made up of many unique prophetic pieces and words all pointing to the same call—to rebuild God's temple.

While Tracy has faithfully embodied and championed this call in her own life, with this call she has courageously invited us to join with her in this sacred journey to awaken hearts to reverent consecration mixed with relevant action leading to cultural reformation and transformation as a rising remnant possessed by purity and passion live out their lives to fulfill the high purposes of God in their day.

It is my joy and honor to not only endorse *God's End-Time Temple* but to even more so endorse and recommend to you the life and ministry of my friend Tracy Eckert, a true prophetic pioneer.

JASON HOOPER
Senior Pastor, King's Way Church
Irondale, Alabama

In the twenty-plus years I've known Tracy, I've been amazed by what I've seen God do in her and through her. In this book she shares several encounters she has had with the Lord, and her detailed accounts will intrigue you in the revelatory perspective that leads to a greater understanding of the Lord and our relationship with Him.

TERRY MOORE
Founding and Lead Pastor, Sojourn Church
Carrollton, Texas

GOD'S END-TIME TEMPLE

The Prophetic Blueprint of Zerubbabel's Temple,
and the Plan to Fill His People with
Glory for Worldwide Awakening

TRACY ECKERT

DESTINY IMAGE® PUBLISHERS, INC.

P.O. Box 310, Shippensburg, PA 17257-0310

"Promoting Inspired Lives."

This book and all other Destiny Image and Destiny Image Fiction books are available at Christian bookstores and distributors worldwide.

Cover art by Casey Parrott: www.caseyparrottart.com

Interior design by Terry Clifton

For more information on foreign distributors, call 717-532-3040.

Reach us on the Internet: www.destinyimage.com.

ISBN 13 TP: 978-0-7684-5424-6

ISBN 13 eBook: 978-0-7684-5425-3

ISBN 13 HC: 978-0-7684-5427-7

ISBN 13 LP: 978-0-7684-5426-0

For Worldwide Distribution, Printed in the U.S.A.

1 2 3 4 5 6 7 8 / 24 23 22 21 20

DEDICATION

I dedicate this book to my beloved husband, John, our seven children, Ryan, Joe, Brecka, Bliss, Ashley, Madison, and Samuel and our Storehouse family. A special thanks to Ann Marie Turner and Matthew Esquivel for helping me write this book. The love and support you all have given me, gave me strength and courage to run my race and journey through the revelation of Zerubbabel's temple.

CONTENTS

FOREWORD

We learn from the Old Testament that when the work of the Lord is suspended, delayed, or perhaps even going in the wrong direction, God raises up prophets like Haggai and Zechariah to prophesy and stir up the spirit of Zerubbabel in the land. We are at a very critical time in history when I believe God is raising up prophetic voices like Tracy Eckert to actually call upon apostles and pioneers to build houses of glory in the earth that can thrive in the midst of global shaking.

As a pioneer, you cannot do the will of God without challenging the way things have always been and causing catalytic changes in the body of Christ. It will also bring about attacks from the devil that many are not ready for. This book contains information, revelation, and prophetic insight to not only instruct those who are on the frontlines on how to build but also keys to defeat the snares of the enemy that can bring weariness and defeat.

As I have walked with Tracy over the last few years, it has been to my delight to discover that she is not only anointed as a prophetic voice but also carries a unique apostolic blueprint that she is revealing in the pages you are about to read. This book is packed with prophetic revelation, an incredible biblical storyline, and the author's own passionate pursuit concerning God's End-Time Temple.

God is definitely calling out to church leadership in this hour, "Consider Your Ways!" (Haggai 1) The COVID-19 era as I call it has made this reality painfully clear to many. The way we have chosen to build God's house is not sufficient for the days ahead. Now is the time for God's end time temple to emerge!

If you are ready to be encouraged by Tracy's candidness regarding her own pioneering journey, and if you are hungry for prophetic strategies and a true apostolic blueprint, this book is for you. It is my pleasure to wholeheartedly not only endorse this end time message, but even more so, the messenger. Tracy Eckert is humble in spirit and exudes the kind of Christ likeness that is so needed in today's leader. May you be refreshed, inspired, and challenged as you read this manuscript. I know I was!

JEREMIAH JOHNSON
Best-selling Author and Speaker
www.jeremiahjohnson.tv

PREFACE

Friend, the book you hold in your hands is the fruit of more than twenty years of prophetic history. Woven throughout its pages is the story of my supernatural salvation where I was encountered by the voice of God with a command, a collection of words, dreams, and encounters recorded before and since the inception of the *House of Zerubbabel,* later renamed *Storehouse.*

Over the years, I have grown increasingly zealous to share what I believe the Lord has in His heart for us through the revelation of Jesus through the story of Zerubbabel who was the heir apparent to the throne of David called to rebuild the second temple and lead the second exodus.

I believe God is saying that He is fully restoring the internal identity of His bride as both priests and kings to God, which is the governmental authority that brings heaven to earth. We are the capstone—last days—generation, followers of Jesus who bring heaven to earth through the plumb line in Zerubbabel's hand. The Lord tells us to write the vision and make it plain so that those who hear it can run with it.

When God speaks prophetically, it is to birth something in the earth. Sometimes He births a message for a few, and sometimes for many. Sometimes for a city, or other times for a nation or nations.

As the bride of Christ, we are living in an extraordinary time in history. Never before have there been the challenges and pressures like those facing our generation. However, never before have there been such extraordinary opportunities to shine as light in the darkness with power and access the deep revelations of God. The Lord promised we would walk in the "greater works" (John 14:12). Indeed, we are a unique generation with a unique mandate, and I believe the final generation alive before the Lord's return.

In Daniel 12:4, the angel told him to seal up the words of his prophecy until "the time of the end," indicating there is end-time, or time-specific, revelation available to us. Not because we're better than, but because we need it given our divine appointment with "the time of the end." For this reason, I believe the Lord is unlocking books of the Bible and sharing end-time-specific prophetic revelation with those willing to search out and discover the treasures of His heart.

This has already been happening. Take, for example, the Song of Solomon. For many years, it was viewed primarily as a book about marriage that celebrates the romantic intimacy between a husband and wife. However in the 1990s, International House of Prayer in Kansas City began releasing fresh understanding in the form of "the bridal paradigm." What happened next was a mass awakening in the Body of Christ to a fresh understanding of the Song of Solomon as a message of love from a Bridegroom God to His bride Church. This has served a great purpose in awakening His bride and establishing us in love. Thankfully, believers around the world have been impacted with heart-empowering revelation of God's affections, and grown in intimacy with Jesus as a result.

In Zechariah chapter 4, a key passage in my own spiritual journey, the prophet is awakened "as a man awakened out of sleep," and the first thing the angel asked him is, "What do you see?" That's an important question for us today, beloved. *What do you see?* I believe the Lord is awakening us in this hour to function as priests with eyes to see and ears to hear from heaven so that as kings, we can release the truth of His purposes in greater measure upon the earth. The fullness of God and apostolic reformation is not either/or but both/and.

As I share with you the insights I've discovered, my prayer is that your heart will be awakened with fresh understanding of what the story of Zerubbabel means for this last generation. I invite you to grab a cup of coffee, find a comfy chair, and kick up your feet. Consider what the Lord is saying to you. As part of God's end-time army, take it personally. There's something He wants to impart to you as you read, preparing you for the days to come. I'm honored to share what I've received.

Thank you for reading,

TRACY ECKERT
Dallas, Texas

PART ONE

PROPHECIES — REBUILD MY TEMPLE

1

THE AWAKENING

God Pulled an Audible...

On August 12, 1999, as I was getting ready for work, something happened that changed the course of my life and the lives of my family forever. I heard the audible voice of God say, *"Rebuild My temple."* I was an unsaved American "Christian" who had no interest in church other than using it as behavioral management for my six teenagers. I had never read the Bible and had no interest in Jesus other than the holidays, Christmas and Easter. But on this day, these three words, "Rebuild My temple," changed the direction and purpose of my life forever. I was so stunned by this experience that I sat there for two hours trying to get my head around what had just happened. His voice was so clear and so profound, and yet I wasn't sure what He meant or how to respond. After all, I'm not Jewish. What do I know about temples?

After God spoke to me, it was like the event stirred up my senses and I began to see in the Spirit. The morning after hearing His voice, just as I was waking, I heard the Lord speak in my spirit, "Rebuild My temple." Then the next morning it happened again. And again. For seven days, the same thing happened. God was telling me to rebuild His temple.

I had no grid for these encounters. I didn't know God spoke, and I didn't know anyone else who had heard His voice. Those three words, "Rebuild My temple," became so heavy on my conscience that I wanted the voice to stop so that my life could return to normal. The Voice, however, only grew louder. Over the next several months I went through an intense season of open revelation with open visions, prophetic dreams, and seeing in the spirit with my natural eyes. Even further over the next fifteen years, He downloaded the building blocks of encounters that created the story you are about to read.

I have been carrying the message of Zerubbabel since 1999. The Lord birthed the revelation of the coming exodus and great awakening through signs in the heavens and on the earth, angelic visitations, dreams, visions, and the audible voice of the Lord. Okay, that's quite a list. You'd think I would have written this book earlier, but I was waiting on the Lord's timing.

Modern-Day Cyrus Appears

In 2015, Lance Wallnau prophesied that the next president would be the United States 45th president, and would be like the Cyrus mentioned in Isaiah 45. I knew when I heard Lance Wallnau's prophecy from his book *God's Chaos Candidate*,[1] about our 45th president being a Cyrus like that of Zerubbabel's temple in Isaiah 45, that this was a sign of the new priesthood that was about to emerge.

This book you are reading is not typical—it is heavy on the prophetic interwoven within its pages. I have broken it down into three sections: prophetic, historical, and revelation. I am going to share much of the prophetic over the next several pages. This is important because God is trying to communicate to us about what He is releasing and how to be prepared to host the habitation of His glory.

Zerubba-WHO?

Zerubba-WHO? I said to myself. WHO is Zerubbabel?

When the Lord first starting speaking to me in 2001 about Zerubbabel and the temple he rebuilt, it was through a dream, actually a *series* of dreams and events. In fact, I'll tell the story in more detail later, but when I first heard his name, I was clueless—I wasn't even sure he was a real person. Quickly, the Lord taught me that Zerubbabel *had* been a real person. In fact, he was a very important leader in the Old Testament, and his life is very significant to us today.

In this book, I share many of the dreams that have spoken to me throughout my journey. Dreams are not the only way that God speaks, but I do believe it's clear throughout Scripture— as was the case with Joseph, Daniel, and the Acts 2 reality with the apostles—that God communicates with us through our dreams. We are not to elevate them above the Word, but it is important to listen to the voice of God as He communicates in this way. I don't pretend to be a biblical scholar, but I do want to share the revelation that the Lord has released through this work, and you can judge for yourself.

The main questions that I originally asked myself, and that I want to answer for you, are:

1. **Who** is Zerubbabel?
2. **What** is the revelation that God is sharing through his life?
3. **How** does God want us to accomplish our call?
4. **Why** is this significant for our generation? And finally,
5. **How** does God want us to live in light of this?

These five questions frame the structure of this book. Whatever your degree of familiarity with our friend Zerubbabel, I invite you to stay with me on this journey. By the end of this book, I'm confident you'll come away with a fresh perspective on his story, our Lord Jesus Christ Himself, the priesthood we're called into, and the glory of what lies ahead for us in these last days.

Let's begin with the story of how the Lord apprehended my life and commissioned me with this life message.

After I heard the audible voice of the Lord say, *"Rebuild My temple,"* a gateway opened to more revelatory encounters.

Open Vision of 9/11

Based on my own self-effort and the wisdom of the world, I had been building a life that the world would consider wealthy and successful, so I was not hungering after God or inviting His presence into my life. When I asked the Voice to go away that was saying, "Rebuild my temple," I was sincere in wanting to go back to my comfort level of being lukewarm. I am *forever grateful* He did not take me up on my request for the voice to leave. Instead, one week into my awakening as I was about to go to sleep, the Holy Spirit came upon me and I began to go into what I now know today was an open vision or trance. My physical body felt heavy like a ghost was keeping me frozen in place. Then everything in front of me disappeared and a real three-dimensional scene began to unfold before my open eyes.

I saw planes exploding over high-rise buildings in New York, and I saw angels and demons fighting over the city. A man whose skin was melting off his bones walked up to me. Covered in ash, he knew he was dying and he looked to his left and, as I followed his gaze, I saw with great horror a pile of dead bodies covered in the same type of ash. I knew I was watching a real event that would happen in the future. When the vision ended, I was in shock. I knew it was coming.

I had this vision in 1999 and by revelation it was clear to me that New York would be attacked and I wrote in my journal: There is something about September 11, 2001 (9/11). I thought to myself, *What in the world is happening to me?* I was jolted into another reality that I didn't know existed. I had no grid for spiritual encounters of any kind. In fact, I'd never heard anyone, not one single person, say that they'd ever heard from God, nor did anyone ever suggest that God still speaks today. A whole new world had opened up to me. It was glorious and shocking at the same time.

It's About Babylon

The following day the Holy Spirit came upon me yet again with the same intensity. I began to cry about what He had shown me happening in New York. I didn't understand why such things would happen, so I asked, "Why is this happening?" He answered, *"It's about Babylon,"* and with open eyes I saw a pentagram pendant on a red velvet ribbon necklace.

There I was in the swirl of these encounters, deeply moved to tears as my husband, John, was waking up beside me. Out loud I asked, "John, John, what's Babylon?" As he arose and thought about it for a few moments, he groggily said, "I don't know, honey, I think it's a tower." Now, this is how uneducated we were in our non-Christian walk—the real-life Dumb and Dumber. I couldn't help but wonder, *God, are You sure that You have the right address here? We know nothing.* Little did I realize that, one day, our unchurched backgrounds would actually work in our favor. Truly, He does all things well.

I went around for two years telling people that we were going to be attacked in New York and they thought I was crazy, but I knew that this was real.

The Tree of Life and 24/7 Prayer

Another dream shortly after this grabbed my attention. In the dream, I see the Statue of Liberty, and it falls into the ocean. I hear the Lord's voice in the dream say, "You haven't taught your sons to battle but I'm raising up another generation...." In the place of the fallen Statue of Liberty I saw many young people who had ropes tied to a tree, and they all began to pull up this tree in the place of the Statue of Liberty. The tree stretched all the way into the heavens. On the trunk of this tree was carved a heart and written inside was, "The Tree of Life." All around it were names of people carved into the tree. While the youth were the primary age group—maybe 20-somethings, teens?—that I saw, there were multiple generations standing around the tree holding it up. They never left the tree. They were around it day and night, 24/7.

Zerubbabel's Baby

Rebuild My temple. 9/11 vision. It's about Babylon. Tree of Life. By this point in my life, my husband, John, and I had thankfully found a great church that was helping us become more grounded in our relationship with the Lord. But we were still unsure as to what God was trying to say through these experiences I was having.

But then came another surprising dream. In the dream, I was pregnant and having difficulty with my pregnancy. I went to get a sonogram. The doctor was the best obstetrician in town and she said that she could help me deliver a healthy baby. While we could see the pictures of the baby, I heard the Lord say, *"The father is Zerubbabel. The father is Zerubbabel. The father is Zerubbabel."*

This may not seem to be all that profound, but this dream marked me. I knew that this was the calling on my life. At the same time, I had no idea who Zerubbabel was—and no idea how to even spell it!

The Holy Spirit is so good because He had already prepared to teach me the very next day. I was praying through a daily Scripture blog from Chuck Pierce, founder of Glory of Zion International Ministries, and the Scripture of the day was from Ezra 5:2 (NLT):

Zerubbabel, son of Shealtiel and Joshua, son of Jehozadak responded by starting again to rebuild the Temple of God in Jerusalem. And the prophets of God were with them and helped them.

Wait a minute. I had to reread this several times. Did Zerubbabel *rebuild the temple*? I could hardly believe what I was reading. This is what God spoke to me when He broke in over me back in 1999. He said, *"Rebuild My temple."* There it was again. I was shocked by the connection but still had no idea what that meant. Why would the God of heaven and earth want an Old Testament temple to be rebuilt?

Worship and Prayer

Another visitation in the coming weeks would help me understand that this "temple" had to do with worship and prayer. One day I had laid down to rest, and immediately I could feel the Holy Spirit come upon me. It felt like my body was levitating. All of the sudden, although I was still in my body, my spirit was in heaven. I looked around and saw fields of flowers and a clear stream of water that were living. Creation was pulsating and teeming with motion, sound, and dimension. I heard a sound that was so incredibly beautiful and melodic. The air was living and responding to the sound.

Jesus walked up to me. His face was like the sun. He had three shadowed men near Him on His right side and two shadowed men on His left side. I asked Him, "What is that sound?" He said, *"That is the prayers of the saints, it gives life to everything you see."* He began to speak to me and tell me the most amazing mysteries. The words were discernible to my mind, but then they were going into my spirit and disappearing. Then the last thing He said, I remembered clearly, *"In the days to come, worship is going to be very important."* Then I was back in my body.

The two things I remember most from our conversation were about the importance of *prayer and worship.*

Next, the Lord told me to go to One Thing Conference in Kansas City, hosted by the International House of Prayer in Kansas City (IHOP-KC). I didn't know anything about IHOP-KC, but I went and took my daughter. When we arrived, the place was infused with the Holy Spirit. Everything about the experience was electric. The atmosphere was filled with His presence. There were beautiful young people everywhere, loving Jesus and loving each other. I heard preaching that powerfully hit my heart. Two men, Mike Bickle, the leader of IHOP, and Lou Engle with TheCall, were so radical. Lou did a rocking thing with his body that was interesting. Their messages were the same as what the Holy Spirit had been telling me about preparing this generation for the return of Jesus. I strangely felt like I had found my home. Somehow these people were my tribe.

Months later in 2002, I ran into Lou Engle at Christ for the Nations Institute (CFNI), and he prophesied to me that I would start the House of Prayer in Dallas, Texas. This was not good news for me. I was excited about going to someone else's house of prayer, but the thought of starting my own was terrifying and daunting. I loved being in the presence of God, but I was no Mike Bickle or Lou Engle who were prayer ninjas. I laughed and told him that I would pray about it. My heavenly inquiry consisted of asking the Lord over a meal that if He wanted us to start the Dallas House of Prayer, to show us in a dream. That night our daughter, Ashley, had this dream:

> We were in a city named Taanach, which was also a training center where we teach people to pray. There was a sign over the door that read: IF YOU TEACH THEM TO PRAY, YOU DON'T HAVE TO TELL THEM HOW TO LIVE.

We knew that was a yes from God, but didn't know how it would happen. I already had the history of Zerubbabel, Babylon, Tree of Life, etc. as a backdrop. God was building a story, but what was He saying? Over the next four years, we continued to carry this prophecy and receive several more confirming words from other prophets. Then in 2006, I stepped into a year of prophetic confirmations that led to the opening of the House of Zerubbabel in Dallas—later changed to Storehouse, since no one can spell Zerubbabel!

A friend sent me a prophetic word from Matt Sorger that was posted on The Elijah List. In this message, the Lord was talking about an awakening through the language and message of Zerubbabel. As I read it, I realized that God is really doing something that will transform the Church in a profound way, resulting in churches with power not just to function in the spiritual gifts, but the glory of God to change whole cities and shift various areas of culture. The repeated messages from the Lord about Zerubbabel, governmental authority, rebuilding the temple, the new priesthood, Babylon, and 24/7 prayer and worship highlight significant themes to us and whoever will listen.

The following is the prophetic word from Matt Sorger posted on The Elijah List in May 2006:

"AWAKENING: THE INVASION OF GOD INTO OUR CULTURE"

Recently, while I was in Texas, covering a lot of territory, I found one ingredient was the same wherever I went. The people were hungry and desperate for a fresh move of God.

The Heart of Texas Will Be Revived— Awakening the Heart of America

The Lord communicated His heart to me in a profound way during my time in Texas. One night, as I stepped to the pulpit, I was instantly caught up into an open-eyed vision. As the Spirit caught me up, I could see the entire state of Texas. Then I saw a large heart beginning to beat stronger and stronger; it was the heart of Texas. The Holy Spirit spoke to me and said, "I am about to revive and awaken the heart of Texas." He said, "When you see the heart of Texas revived, the heart of the nation will be revived as well." In the midst of this vision I realized that Texas held a key to releasing national revival in America.

We are about to see Texas visited with a mighty move of the Holy Spirit. As the heart of the Church is revived and awakened in Texas, it will then cause an Awakening to hit the entire nation of America; turning the heart of our nation toward God.

Governmental Authority Is Being Given to Reverse the Death Culture

Dallas is a key city in Texas. There is a governmental authority God is giving to Dallas to reverse the death culture that was released over our nation in Roe v. Wade back in 1973. As the heart of Texas is revived, we will see a reversal of this death culture and the Spirit of Life released over our nation. Dallas, Texas, is a key city for prophetic decrees to be released and to see a breakthrough in the Supreme Court of America.

Three Groups Will Be Visited: Government Leaders, Spiritual Leaders, and the Remnant

As Awakening is released in our nation, not only will it revive and renew the Church, but we will also see a shift come as society begins to be radically impacted by this move of God. This anointing and outpouring will reach into many areas of society and bring great Kingdom transformation.

Haggai 1:7,8,14 and Haggai 2:1-9, are key scriptures for the Awakening that is upon us. God speaks through the prophet Haggai, for the people to consider their ways and to rebuild God's temple, so that He may be glorified. In Haggai 1:14, the Lord "stirred up" the spirit of Zerubbabel (the governor of Judah, and the high priest, Joshua, and the remnant of the people), they came and worked on (rebuilt) the house of the Lord so that God could have a temple in which to dwell. As the prophetic voice was released, there was a supernatural stirring that took place. In Hebrew the phrase "to stir" is ur. It means "to awaken, to stir up, to excite, to raise up, to arouse to action, to open one's eyes." It means "to awaken someone from sleep and rouse them to a place of action." This awakening hits three groups of people: the governor, the high priest, and the remnant. The Lord showed me that there will be three groups of people hit with this Awakening: political leaders, spiritual leaders, and the remnant in the Church.

We will see the prophetic word of the Lord invade the government arena as God opens doors for His servants to prophesy the word of the Lord to government leaders. God's Spirit will even invade the Oval Office of the White House as well as the Supreme Court. Many other political leaders will receive divine encounters as God's heart is shared with them. We will also see the hearts of many spiritual leaders across our nation and the world stirred with a fresh moving of the Holy Spirit. Their main ambition in ministry will be to build a habitation for God's glory in the earth through His Church.

We will also see the remnant of God's people arise in this hour to offer their lives in a new and deeper way as a living habitation for God's presence and glory. Kingdom pursuits will become much more important and prioritized than just living a comfortable lifestyle. People will even be willing to sacrifice, so that God's glory can have a dwelling place in the earth through their lives.

Guard Against False Comparison and Discouragement

As God's glory is outpoured and fills His house again, we must be careful not to compare what God does today with what has happened in the past. He gave me a prophetic warning not to fall into false comparison. In Haggai 2:3, the Lord saw that the people were comparing the temple God was calling them to rebuild, to what it was in its former glory in Solomon's day. Haggai 2:3 says, "Is this not in your eyes as nothing?" They remembered how glorious Solomon's temple was; how the cloud had filled the temple so that the priests could no longer continue ministering (2 Chronicles 5:14). An internal enemy of discouragement through false comparison was trying to hinder them from building God's temple.

As God calls us to build a habitation for His glory, we must be careful not to put God nor how He moves into a "revival box." God may show up in a way that is very different than our preconceived ideas. We must be careful not to fall into a false comparison (even with past moves of God), and allow God to release His greater glory in the way

He wants to do it. We must stay open and sensitive to the Holy Spirit so we don't miss Him when He comes.

Greater Glory and Supernatural Provision

Haggai prophesies in Haggai 2:4-9, "'Yet now be strong...and work; for I am with you. ...Once more...I will shake heaven and earth, the sea and dry land; and I will shake all nations and they shall come to the Desire of All Nations, and I will fill this temple with glory.... The silver is Mine, and the gold is Mine.... The glory of this latter temple shall be greater than the former...and in this place I will give peace,' says the Lord of hosts."

His promise is that no matter what the temple looks like on the outside, the glory shall be greater on the inside! He also throws in there a promise for continual divine provision to get the job done. God reaffirms that all the gold and silver are His; He owns it all. We will see a great supernatural provision for the Church to build God's Kingdom in the earth; building a place for His greater glory to dwell.

God Will Invade Our Society, in Politics and Media

There is a greater glory upon us. Awakening is about to hit America and the nations on many levels including both spiritual and political. As political leaders catch the heart of God, they will begin to rally causes that are on God's heart. This is where we will begin to see the walls broken down once again between Church and State. Not only will the Church be set on fire, but society will be impacted through righteous political leaders. We will also see an invasion of God into the media. Jesus is about to be glorified in Hollywood and through the media, both secular and Christian. New networks will be formed that will glorify God. Churches must be prepared to take the airwaves for God as a new wave of media outreach and anointing is upon us.

This next Awakening will shake the Church and bring a great transformation in our culture and society as the Holy Spirit empowers us to reach the world with His supernatural grace and power.

After John and I read this word from Matt, we thought, *Oh no, we're going to have to do this house of prayer thing.* This word confirmed what I was hearing from the Lord in a very profound and meaningful way. This is really the word that hit me like a freight train and made me realize that we had a tiger by the tail. So John and I prayed and agreed that we wanted all that God had for us on this side of eternity.

I expected the house of prayer that the Lord was telling us to start to look much like IHOP-KC, but the Lord showed me through another dream that we would have a unique expression message that would point to the type of authority He was releasing on His praying church around the world.

Dream: Governmental Authority

I had a dream where I am standing in the IHOP-KC prayer room looking at the Scripture on the east wall from Ezekiel 44:15: *"The priests, the sons of Zadok, who kept charge of My sanctuary, they shall come near to Me to minister to Me."* As I stood there, I heard the Lord say, *"You are not Zadok priests, you are the House of Zerubbabel, governmental authority."*

The next day, I received an email from Lou Engle that read, "You are the house of governmental authority, the house of Zerubbabel but you are priests too."

I took two things from this dream. First of all, I knew that the model of the house of prayer that the Lord was telling us to start would look very similar to IHOP-KC, but we would also have a unique expression. Second, in the bigger picture, the end-time temple that Zerubbabel's temple signifies would operate in not only a priestly ministry, but a kingly ministry, and the two combined is called governmental authority.

I did not understand what the term "governmental authority" meant, but I knew it had to do with influence in the spirit and power on our words. Though I will unpack this more fully later in the book, I will say this right now: while we are functioning in a measure of authority on our declarations, there is coming a double portion of grace on our intercession so powerful that I believe it will usher in an awakening, shake nations, and beckon Jesus back to the earth.

Piecing it all Together

From the moment God's voice came to get me, He has been prophetically building a story about the rebuilding of His temple according to the New Covenant priesthood in Christ Jesus. So how do the building blocks of these encounters fit together?

1. "Rebuild My temple": This is Zerubbabel's temple, which I believe was an Old Testament picture of the New Testament temple of Christ in man, which will not be a *physical* temple built with human hands, but a *spiritual* temple built by God Himself. He is rebuilding us as living stones into His spiritual house to carry His glory like never before.

> *You also, like living stones, are being built into a spiritual house, to be a holy priesthood, offering spiritual sacrifices acceptable to God through Jesus Christ* (1 Peter 2:5 NIV).
>
> *To them God willed to make known what are the riches of the glory of this mystery among the Gentiles: which is Christ in you, the hope of glory* (Colossians 1:27).

2. Vision of 9/11: God showed me two key verses related to 9/11 and the rebuilding of this New Testament temple. It will contain the spirit of worship and prayer like the tabernacle of David, but it will operate in the order of Jesus Christ our High Priest and Intercessor. The Book of Hebrews calls this ministry of Jesus "the order of Melchizedek."

> *On that day I will raise up the tabernacle of David,*
> *which has fallen down, and repair its damages; I*
> *will raise up its ruins, and rebuild it as in the days*
> *of old* (Amos 9:11).
>
> *But Christ came as High Priest of the good things to*
> *come, with the greater and more perfect tabernacle*
> *not made with hands, that is, not of this creation*
> (Hebrews 9:11).
>
> *Where the forerunner has entered for us, even Jesus,*
> *having become High Priest forever according to the*
> *order of Melchizedek* (Hebrews 6:20).

3. "It's About Babylon": Zerubbabel led the Jews out of Babylon. God is taking His Church today out of a spiritual Babylon and opening our eyes. He will rebuild this chosen generation into His *holy* temple and into a *holy* priesthood—called out of darkness into light, and unstained by the wisdom of the world.

> *And I heard another voice from heaven saying,*
> *"Come out of her [Babylon], my people, lest you*
> *share in her sins, and lest you receive of her plagues"*
> (Revelation 18:4).
>
> *But you are a chosen generation, a royal priesthood,*
> *a holy nation, His own special people, that you may*
> *proclaim the praises of Him who called you out of*
> *darkness into His marvelous light* (1 Peter 2:9).

4. Tree of Life Lifted Up 24/7: In the past twenty years, prayer rooms have exploded worldwide with young adults giving themselves to night and day prayer. Whereas this New

Testament temple will consist of all generations, God is highlighting the role of young adults who will usher in a movement of continual prayer and worship around the world.

> *"For from the rising of the sun, even to its going down, My name shall be great among the Gentiles; in every place incense shall be offered to My name, and a pure offering; for My name shall be great among the nations," says the LORD of hosts* (Malachi 1:11).

5. Birthing Zerubbabel's Baby: Zerubbabel rebuilt the second temple. The anointing that was on Zerubbabel to rebuild the second temple is coming to the present-day Church to rebuild God's living temple of Christ in us.

> *Now, therefore, you are no longer strangers and foreigners, but fellow citizens with the saints and members of the household of God, having been built on the foundation of the apostles and prophets, Jesus Christ Himself being the chief cornerstone, in whom the whole building, being fitted together, grows into a holy temple in the Lord, in whom you also are being built together for a dwelling place of God in the Spirit* (Ephesians 2:19-22).

6. Taken to Heaven, Prayer and Worship: This temple that God is rebuilding involves worship and the prayers of the saints that will bring the life of heaven to the earth.

> *Now when He had taken the scroll, the four living creatures and the twenty-four elders fell down*

before the Lamb, each having a harp, and golden bowls full of incense, which are the prayers of the saints. And they sang a new song... (Revelation 5:8-9).

Your kingdom come, Your will be done, on earth as it is in heaven (Matthew 6:10).

7. Awakening and Governmental Authority: The Church will operate in governmental authority that will bring in an awakening and cultural transformation. I was seeing 2:22 and 22:22 everywhere and all the time. I knew this was the Holy Spirit speaking about Isaiah 22:22, the authority that David was given. This kind of authority will rest on the Church and exponentially increase the power on our intercession and declarations.

The key of the house of David I will lay on his shoulder; so he shall open, and no one shall shut; and he shall shut, and no one shall open (Isaiah 22:22).

These dreams, prophecies, and visions moved me and John from arguing with God about starting a house of prayer to saying yes and asking how, when, etc. We knew this would change the landscape of our family and the trajectory of our lives. We weren't exactly sure what to do with it. But more signs and wonders would follow to guide us.

Endnote

1. Lance Wallnau, *God's Chaos Candidate: Donald J. Trump and the American Unraveling* (Keller, TX: Killer Sheep Media, Inc., 2016).

2

SIGNS AND WONDERS

*I will show wonders in heaven above and signs in the
earth beneath: blood and fire and vapor of smoke.*
—Acts 2:19

The Next Great Awakening

As you can see from the last chapter, God has been using
the language of *awakening* throughout His prophetic words,
dreams, and visions. It is the same language He used with
Zerubbabel in the actual temple he rebuilt. The reality is we
have been born in the most extraordinary time in history. We
are on the precipice of the greatest awakening in the history of
the world. Never before have there been the challenges, pressures, and lawlessness like those facing our generation. We are
about to witness a massive exodus of billions of people out of
the system of the world and into the system of the Kingdom
of heaven.

We are what the great cloud of witnesses have been waiting
for and the fulfillment of what they never fully realized. There

will be such extraordinary opportunities to shine as light in the darkness with power and love, accessing the deep revelations of God's heart and dreams. God is using the compilation of prophecies and revelation about Zerubbabel's temple to rebuild His people to host His coming glory.

In the last chapter, we discussed the supernatural encounters that God used to communicate the importance of Zerubbabel's temple to the Church that will usher in the return of the Lord. In this chapter, I share messages given through angelic encounters, through Jesus appearing, and through signs in the heavens and on earth. These signs and wonders further communicate the importance of God speaking to our generation through these profound encounters.

Angelic Encounters

In addition to Matt Sorger's word about Zerubbabel, I became aware of three angelic encounters that occurred in 2006-2008:

1. My friend Rick Pino was visited by the angel of Zechariah 4, which is the angel that gave the message to Zerubbabel through the prophet Zechariah, who said, *"It's time to awaken."*

2. Pastor Steven Shelley of New Hope Revival Ministries in Alabama was visited by angel who announced, *"The plumb line is now in the hand of Zerubbabel."*[1]

3. Jeff Jansen of Global Fire Ministries had a visitation from Jesus who said, *"The plumb line is now in the hand of Zerubbabel."*[2]

The series of encounters I had personally made it clear to me that the significance of Zerubbabel's temple was bigger than a local prayer ministry in Dallas that God was telling my husband and I to start. I was encouraged to hear more prophetic people including Matt Sorger, Rick Pino, Steven Shelly, and Jeff Jansen talking about Zerubbabel. What gripped me was that these were men with established ministries who had a history of prophetic accuracy and credibility. None of them knew anything about the dreams, visions, and prophecies I was receiving about Zerubbabel. Reading about what the Lord had spoken to them about Zerubbabel confirmed to me that the Lord was trying to communicate something to our generation. The Lord, however, decided to put yet another exclamation point on this message with 1) His audible voice and 2) signs in the heavens and on earth.

Audible Voice

The Truth Starts Now: One day in 2006 while I was making my bed and cleaning my bedroom, I heard thunder but it was also a voice that said, *"The truth starts now."* This thunder was so loud that it shook my house. I was stunned and sat down in awe and wonder. I am amazed by God's ways. I don't always understand, but He has been faithful to later bring the understanding. I was wondering why, if God is going to the trouble to speak audibly, why would He say something that seemed so generic and unconnected to His messages about Zerubbabel's temple. It felt like a departure from the themes around the rebuilding of the temple.

It was many years later when I asked Paul Keith Davis about the meaning of the plumb line in Zechariah 4. He told me that it is the *truth* from heaven to earth. There was the connection! God wasn't randomly speaking, He was adding meaning to the mystery of the story He was telling. This was very exciting. He told me that the plumb line that laid the foundation of the temple is being released again to finish the work with the capstone (more on the capstone in a later chapter).

Let My People Go: God's voice thundered again (literally) in 2007, but this time I was not the one who heard it. My 7-year-old son, Samuel, did. Samuel and I were leaving the house one day with his sitter. Not a cloud in the sky. Our front door was standing open, and suddenly a clap of thunder shook the house. All the car alarms in the street went off. The babysitter and I looked at each other and said, "What in the world is that?!" Young Samuel grabbed me and said, "Mom! Mom! God just said, 'Let My people go!'" Again, I just stood there amazed and shocked but not really understanding the message. Later, the mystery was unlocked when I understood God was saying that there was coming another exodus just like there was with Zerubbabel. Remember: *It's about Babylon.* God was taking His people out of a Babylonian state of confusion and bringing them into a life of hearing and releasing His truth into the earth.

Signs in the Heavens

As we started the Dallas House of Prayer, no one came except me. There I would be in the little side living room of my house praying. Alone. I thought to myself, *Lord, this doesn't look like a house of prayer!* My reluctance to start a house of prayer was due to the fact that I really didn't know how to pray and I didn't understand that prayer could be enjoyable, even heavenly. I loved the presence of the Lord and I loved being in the IHOP-KC prayer room, but my daily prayer life was difficult.

The Lord told me to begin with twelve hours per week of prayer in three-hour segments. My cry was, "Lord, teach me to pray!" I am a German extrovert who loves activity and work. I have a very loud soul life. So in the beginning of these prayer times, I was hurting a little with the silence and perceived boredom. What I didn't understand was the exchange that was happening. My spirit life was growing louder and my soul life—mind, will, emotions—was waning. I began to have encounters with the Lord that were wrecking my heart with love and encouragement. I was not alone in prayer—I had the God of the universe speaking over and to me.

Vision of Supreme Court

That same summer of 2007, as I was praying in that little prayer room, I was taken into an open-eyed vision. I saw a heart over Washington, DC. The heart squeezed down into a pipe that was connected to the foundation of America.

I had a friend who worked with the Justice House of Prayer (JHOP) in Washington, DC, who had a team of youth praying in front of the Supreme Court, partnering with Bound4Life LIFE campaign. I called her and explained the vision. The next day, while she was praying in front of the Supreme Court, the most remarkable sign in the heavens appeared right in front of her and she snapped a picture of it on her phone. A cloud in the shape of a heart formed over the Supreme Court and practically touched the tip.

Remember what Matt Sorger had prophesied, "I am about to revive and awaken the heart of Texas." He said, "When *you see the heart of Texas revived, the heart of the nation* will be revived as well…. As the heart of Texas is revived, we will see a reversal of this death culture and the Spirit of Life released over our nation. Dallas, TX is a key city for prophetic decrees to be released and to see a breakthrough in the Supreme Court of America."

Signs on the Earth

Several months later, we began to notice bugs on one side of our front yard. They are chinch bugs that eat Bermuda grass in Texas. They chewed small circles of grass, and over a period of a couple of weeks, I noticed that all these small circles were connecting. Finally one day, I saw that these little connected circles made the shape of a heart. I couldn't believe my eyes. Nowhere else on my lawn were there any circles from these bugs. We went onto the roof of our house and took this picture.

So like me, you may be asking, "What in the world?" We've seen a heart in the sky and now one in my yard. A sign in the heavens and a sign on earth. I think it is hilarious that God commanded these bugs to chew a heart in my yard. So bizarre! And by the way, we never put any treatment on these bugs and they never chewed beyond this heart shape; and soon afterward, it disappeared.

I believe God is putting His initials on Matt Sorger's prophecy about "when you see the heart of Texas awakened, the heart of America will be awakened" through the message that He gave to Haggai and Zechariah for Zerubbabel over 2,500 years ago. So the question is: what could He be releasing on the earth once again that He is intent on seeing birthed?

Endnotes

1. Steven L. Shelley, "Angels with Assignment Are Preparing Us to Receive Perhaps the Most Astounding Revelation of All Time—From the Open Book," *The Elijah List*, September 22, 2009; http://www.elijahlist.com/words/display_word.html ?ID=8046; accessed July 15, 2020.

2. Jeff and Jan Jansen, "Synchronizing Heaven and Earth—The Plumb Line in the Hand of Zerubbabel," *The Elijah List*, June 17, 2009; http://www.elijahlist.com/words/display_word .html?ID=7744; accessed July 15, 2020.

PART TWO

HISTORICAL PERSPECTIVE—
THE BIG PICTURE

Zerubbabel's rebuilt temple is the prophetic symbol of the New Testament temple housing a different kind of priest— the priesthood of Melchizedek functioning as both king and priest, the government of God within humans.

3

ZERUBBA, WHO?

And after they were brought to Babylon, Jeconiah
begot Shealtiel, and Shealtiel begot Zerubbabel.
—Matthew 1:12

From this point forward, I will be writing from the historical perspective of Zerubbabel then and how it applies today. The Old Testament has within it patterns, shadows that prophesy about the real that came with Jesus' generation and is coming through the last generation.

As I mentioned, when the Lord started speaking to me about Zerubbabel, I had no idea who this man was, how to spell his name, or even if he was a real person. Much less why he was significant to the church in our generation. These personal encounters and the subsequent prophetic words given by others in the Body of Christ alerted me that there was something of great importance regarding Zerubbabel that I needed not only to understand but also to communicate to the Body of Christ.

Hopefully, your heart has been stirred to ask more fervently, "So who is Zerubbabel and why is he important?" In this section I introduce to you the historical Zerubbabel we see in the Old Testament and the role he played in rebuilding the second temple. In Part Three I introduce you to how the revelation of Zerubbabel's temple applies to you and this generation.

So who was Zerubbabel? Zerubbabel is from the tribe of Judah. He is listed in both the lineage of Mary and Joseph in the genealogy of Jesus. He led the second exodus of Israel and built the second temple with Joshua, the high priest, and the remnant of Jews that returned to Jerusalem from captivity.

We know of Moses who led the *first* exodus of Israel out of *Egyptian* captivity. Zerubbabel led the *second* exodus of Israel hundreds of years later out of *Babylonian* captivity, about a thousand years later. We know of David and Solomon who oversaw the construction of the *first* temple, which had been destroyed after the Babylonian invasion of Jerusalem in 587 BC. Zerubbabel, a direct descendent of King David, oversaw the construction of the *second* temple upon the exiles' return to Jerusalem. Quite a résumé considering he grew up in Babylon.

It's interesting to me that many know of the first exodus that Moses led and the first temple that David and Solomon built; yet Zerubbabel, who both led the second exodus *and* built the second temple, is unknown. But God is highlighting this man and his significance to this generation.

A generation prior to their return to Jerusalem under Zerubbabel and Joshua, the people of Judah had been forcibly taken to slave camps in the land of Babylon under the reign of King Nebuchadnezzar, who invaded Jerusalem and destroyed the temple of Solomon in 587 BC. There the people of Judah remained in captivity for 70 years, as the prophet Jeremiah predicted, because of their insistent rebellion against the Lord and their worship of false gods.

However, as the 70 years came to a close, the Babylonians were conquered by the Medo-Persian empire led by Cyrus of Persia and Darius of Media. At the turn of the 70 years, King Cyrus issued a decree that released the captives of Judah to return to Jerusalem and rebuild the Jewish temple under Zerubbabel and Joshua's leadership. Not only were the Jews legally permitted to do this, but Cyrus financed the journey and the construction of this second temple with funds from the Persian empire's treasury. He even sent the sacred objects of the temple that King Nebuchadnezzar's army had stolen 70 years earlier.

Zerubbabel was given the title of the Governor of Judah by King Cyrus. Zerubbabel is not only in the line of King David but also in the genealogy of Jesus. His grandfather, Jeconiah, former king of Judah, and his father, Shealtiel (as a boy), were taken into Babylonian captivity by King Nebuchadnezzar of Babylon. Zerubbabel was of royal blood, and he was the next in line to be king. Under a decree by King Cyrus of Persia, he and Joshua, the high priest of Israel, led a remnant of Jews out of Babylonian slave camps back to Jerusalem. The people who followed them saw this exodus from Babylon as the restoration of the kingdom of Israel, and the golden years of the throne of David would be restored and the Babylonians destroyed.

Now that we have briefly covered the historical period of Zerubbabel's time, let's talk about his name. Hebrew names carry great significance, especially those of key figures in Israel's history. Even Zerubbabel's Babylonian name "Sheshbazzar," given to him by his Babylonian slave masters, gives us insight into the character of this man. The book of Ezra, which charts this period of history, refers to Zerubbabel by the Babylonian name, Sheshbazzar (Ezra 1:8). I mention this because Sheshbazzar means "worshipper of fire." Though the Babylonians likely intended to name him after one of their own gods, I believe the Holy Spirit uses even this pagan name to tell us that this man was an exceptional Jew who was fiery in his zeal, in his dedication, his obedience, and his worship of Yahweh.

Zerubbabel's father knew the promise of the return of the Jews to the land of Israel. He named his son for his life's mission: To lead God's people from Babylonian captivity to rebuild the temple. Many have said that Zerubbabel means "seed of Babylon" but if we look at the Hebraic etymology, we see a deeper meaning.

According to the Hebrew and Chaldee Lexicon to the Old Testament Scriptures (Gesenius), Zerubbabel is a combination of two words: *zerub* and *babel*. Definition of *zerub*: sown in Babylon (Heb. 2216). Zerub: wax warm (Heb. 2215). The meaning of the root word Zerub is regarded by Gesenius as most probable *"to perish, to be dissipated, to pour out, to flow off, or away, used of rivers at the time that they become narrow."* Definition of *babel*: confusion.

Therefore, I believe the truer meaning of his name is to *flow away from confusion.* The way out of confusion and into truth was narrow, yet Zerubbabel believed against all odds as he led the faithful remnant back to Israel that he would rebuild the temple and institute true worship again.

Modern-Day Cyrus Appears

During Donald Trump's presidential campaign, a man named Lance Wallnau prophesied that Trump was like a Cyrus from Isaiah 45, and that he would become the 45th president of the United States. Lance Wallnau has had an established ministry for some time now, but his prophecy about Trump and his book, *God's Chaos Candidate,* certainly caused a lot of controversy. Turns out Wallnau was right about Trump being elected, and I believe he is also right about him being a type of Cyrus regarding Zerubbabel's temple in Isaiah 45. On top of this, the 70th anniversary of Israel becoming a nation was approaching. Remember, Israel was in Babylonian captivity for 70 years. Then in that 70th year, God raised up a Cyrus to bring them out of captivity. To bring them out of the land of confusion and to rebuild the temple for worship and prayer.

When I heard Lance Wallnau's prophecy, I knew that we had entered the timing of the Lord to rebuild and get ready to fulfill all that He has been speaking for almost twenty years. Many have disagreed with—and have even been appalled and enraged by—Donald Trump. However you feel about our 45th president, we need to pay attention to this prophetic message and what God is doing in this hour. It is important because God is trying to communicate to us about what He is releasing and how to be prepared to host His coming glory.

4

LOOKING BACK

Biblical history is a great teacher that lends understanding for future growth.

If I am going to talk to you about the prophetic significance of the second temple built in 516 BC by Zerubbabel, then I think it is helpful to have an understanding of the Old Testament timeline. There are a few major periods of biblical history that come before Zerubbabel's time:

- The Pre-Flood Era (Adam to Noah)
- The Patriarchal Period (Abraham, Isaac, and Jacob)
- Israel's First Exodus (Slavery in Egypt, the leadership of Moses, the Exodus from Egypt, the Ten Commandments, and the wilderness wanderings)
- The Conquest of Canaan (The time of Joshua and Israel's transition into the Promised Land)
- The Period of the Judges (Samson, Deborah, Jephthah, and others)

- The Kingdom of Israel (Saul, David, and Solomon)
- The Divided Kingdom (The split between Judah and Israel)
- The Babylonian Exile (King Nebuchadnezzar's conquest of Jerusalem and 70 years of Judah's captivity in Babylon)

Following the golden years of David and then of his son Solomon, the kingdom of Israel and the kingdom of Judah were divided into two kingdoms that would be led by a series of kings who did evil in the Lord's sight. Occasionally, Judah had kings faithful to the Lord like Hezekiah, Josiah, and others. But for the most part, the kings of both Israel and Judah turned away from the Lord's commands. They departed from the *truth* of His Word.

Therefore, God began to send prophets to give them words of warning. To lead them back to His commands. To lead them back to the truth of His Word. In His love and mercy, the Lord tried warning His people over and over again of the inevitable captivity that results in forsaking Him. (Remember, the Lord said to me, the "Truth begins now." God is sending prophetic messengers today to lead His people back to the truth.)

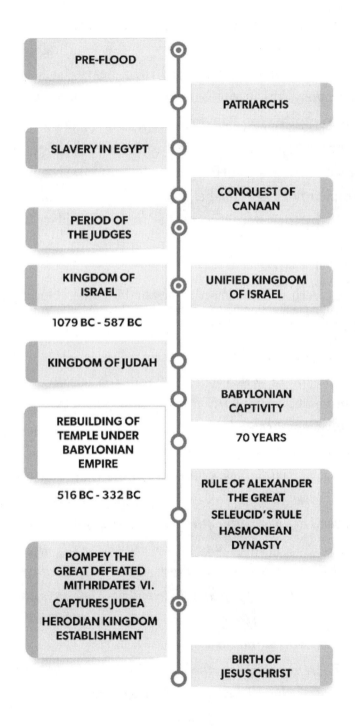

PRE-FLOOD

PATRIARCHS

SLAVERY IN EGYPT

CONQUEST OF CANAAN

PERIOD OF THE JUDGES

KINGDOM OF ISRAEL

UNIFIED KINGDOM OF ISRAEL

1079 BC - 587 BC

KINGDOM OF JUDAH

BABYLONIAN CAPTIVITY

REBUILDING OF TEMPLE UNDER BABYLONIAN EMPIRE

70 YEARS

516 BC - 332 BC

RULE OF ALEXANDER THE GREAT

SELEUCID'S RULE

HASMONEAN DYNASTY

POMPEY THE GREAT DEFEATED MITHRIDATES VI. CAPTURES JUDEA

HERODIAN KINGDOM ESTABLISHMENT

BIRTH OF JESUS CHRIST

He sent the prophets, like Isaiah, Jeremiah, and others, to speak to Israel and tell them of the pending captivity unless they repented and turned their hearts back to Him. Unfortunately, the people's hearts were hard, so God sent them into captivity in Babylon.

In order to understand the historical and prophetic significance of Israel's return to Jerusalem and the rebuilding of the temple under Zerubbabel, it is helpful to look more specifically at why they were in captivity in the first place. In what way had Israel forsaken God that caused Him to discipline them for 70 years?

1.   Rejecting God's Word: They had forsaken God and His words and began worshipping other gods. They built altars and idols to other gods.

> *"And the Lord has sent to you all His servants the prophets, rising early and sending them, but you have not listened nor inclined your ear to hear. They said, 'Repent now everyone of his evil way and his evil doings, and dwell in the land that the Lord has given to you and your fathers forever and ever. Do not go after other gods to serve [obey] them and worship them, and do not provoke Me to anger with the works of your hands; and I will not harm you.' Yet you have not listened to Me," says the Lord, "that you might provoke Me to anger with the works of your hands to your own hurt.*
>
> *"Therefore thus says the Lord of hosts: 'Because you have not heard My words, behold, I will send and take all the families of the north,' says the Lord, 'and*

Nebuchadnezzar the king of Babylon, My servant, and will bring them against this land, against its inhabitants, and against these nations all around, and will utterly destroy them, and make them an astonishment, a hissing, and perpetual desolations. Moreover, I will take from them the voice of mirth and the voice of gladness, the voice of the bridegroom and the voice of the bride, the sound of the millstones and the light of the lamp. And this whole land shall be a desolation and an astonishment, and these nations shall serve the king of Babylon seventy years.

"'Then it will come to pass, when seventy years are completed, that I will punish the king of Babylon and that nation, the land of the Chaldeans, for their iniquity,' says the Lord; 'and I will make it a perpetual desolation'" (Jeremiah 25:4-12).

2. Shedding Innocent Blood: They built an altar to the god of Molech and were sacrificing their babies by searing them with fire on the hands of the burning altar. God, Maker of heaven and earth who knows the beginning from the end makes an incredible statement through Jeremiah:

Because they have forsaken Me and made this an alien place, because they have burned incense in it to other gods whom neither they, their fathers, nor the kings of Judah have known, and have filled this place with the blood of the innocents (they have also built the high places of Baal, to burn their sons with fire for burnt offerings to Baal, which I did not command or speak, nor did it come into My mind) (Jeremiah 19:4-5).

God said, *"...nor did it come into My mind."* God who knows all never imagined such depravity that His chosen people would torture and kill their own children.

So, *obeying/worshipping other gods* and *shedding innocent blood* were the two primary sins that caused the hand of God to move and discipline Israel so they would turn their hearts back to Him.

Even though God was bringing judgment, He did not leave them without hope and a future. After King Nebuchadnezzar conquered Jerusalem, burned down the temple, and carried the people away as captives into Babylon, God instructs them how to live in Babylon, and He gives them a promise that they will return both to Him and to their land.

> *Build houses and dwell in them; plant gardens and eat their fruit. Take wives and beget sons and daughters; and take wives for your sons and give your daughters to husbands, so that they may bear sons and daughters—that you may be increased there, and not diminished. ...For thus says the Lord: After seventy years are completed at Babylon, I will visit you and perform My good word toward you, and cause you to return to this place. For I know the thoughts that I think toward you, says the Lord, thoughts of peace and not of evil, to give you a future and a hope. Then you will call upon Me and go and pray to Me, and I will listen to you. And you*

*will seek Me and find Me, when you search for Me
with all your heart* (Jeremiah 29:5-6,10-13).

Even though there are wilderness experiences as part of
our journey, God leaves us with hope through prophetic promises. Jesus' desire for us is to have hope for our future. Hope is
one of the invisible attributes that makes our future possible.

Return to the stronghold [which is Jesus], *you prisoners of hope. Even today I declare that I will restore
double to you* (Zechariah 9:12).

The thing about hope is that is comes with a promise. A
promise fills us with hope; but when life circumstances do not
seem to line up with that promise, we can easily become dis-
couraged. Hope is an invisible attribute but necessary in order
to partner with the purpose of God for your life. In their time
of distress, their captivity in Babylon, Israel needed, just like
we do today, the following four elements in order to be sus-
tained in the wilderness season and to realize their purpose
through the words of God:

1. A vision and a promise
2. The will to build and love people through the
   process
3. Stay in *hope* that the promise will happen
4. Have faith during the journey

Even though God is sending them into a seventy-year time
out, He leaves His beloved children with hope through words
that will sustain them. God is the same yesterday, today, and

forever. The writer of Hebrews addresses this condition of standing in hope in Hebrews 10:35-36:

> *Therefore do not cast away your confidence, which has a great reward. For you have need of endurance, so that after you have done the will [word] of God, you may receive the promise,*

When the children of Israel were led away into Babylon (confusion), they didn't lose hope because they had the Word of God that kept them believing for their return to the Promised Land.

5

LEAVING BABYLON

The Nature of Biblical Exoduses

The nature of historic biblical exoduses have all had similar elements. The Hebrew word *yatsa* means to go out or go forth like a plant that germinates and expands (Gesenius). All biblical exoduses have been against all odds and are set within difficult political and cultural conditions where God's people are at their weakest, believing but barely holding on.

Zerubbabel's Exodus

In the historical book of Ezra, God fulfills His promises of returning His people to Jerusalem through the leadership of Zerubbabel at the 70th year in 536 BC. King Nebuchadnezzar is overthrown by Cyrus of Persia. During the first year of King Cyrus' reign, the Lord stirred up his spirit and the king proclaimed in all his kingdom:

> *Thus says Cyrus king of Persia: All the kingdoms*
> *of the earth the Lord God of heaven has given me.*
> *And He has commanded me to build Him a house*
> *at Jerusalem which is in Judah. Who is among you*

of all His people? May the Lord his God be with him, and let him go up! (2 Chronicles 36:23)

This is a fulfillment of the words of the prophet Isaiah 150 years before Cyrus was even born:

Who says of Cyrus, "He is My shepherd, and he shall perform all My pleasure, saying to Jerusalem, 'You shall be built,' and to the temple, 'Your foundation shall be laid'" (Isaiah 44:28).

Cyrus further proclaims that all the articles of Solomon's temple that Nebuchadnezzar captured would be given to Zerubbabel who was leading the small remnant of returning Jews. Then he commanded all the people of the land to give them silver, gold, and livestock toward rebuilding the house of the Lord.

This is an incredible proclamation because Cyrus is not Jewish but a Persian king who worships idols and hosts orgies. This is proof that it doesn't matter who is in political office or the condition of leaders of the land. The greatest shifts in God's Kingdom have happened while the most imperfect leaders were in the land: Moses with Pharaoh; David with Saul; Zerubbabel with Cyrus; and Jesus with Herod. I mentioned Lance Wallnau's prophecy about Donald Trump being a modern-day Cyrus. I am not saying—and I don't think Lance Wallnau is either—that our current president mirrors the corruption of Herod or Pharaoh. I am saying that God will open or shut the hearts of people for His purposes and glory.

It was time for the Word of God, the prophecy, to be fulfilled. The time of the 70 years in captivity is over and Cyrus has given the decree to go; but we still have the issue of the children of Israel. What will they do? Has their time as slaves in Babylon changed them? Are they ready for the sacrifice of rebuilding the temple, rebuilding their own homes, and returning to live in their homeland. Do they have the faith and courage to believe God to cross over into the Promised Land, a new way of life and freedom? They returned under the leadership of a man named Zerubbabel, who was the next in line to be crowned king, and Joshua the high priest.

There was a remnant of the entire population that chose to return to Israel and rebuild the temple. Zerubbabel led the first group of 42,360 Jews, 7,337 servants, 200 men, and women singers. They were going to Israel that was populated with Babylonians. They went to rebuild their temple in the midst of their enemy. Their land was occupied, so how would they respond?

Today's Exodus

So what is the significance of this for the Church? I believe that God is leading the remnant of His people through yet another exodus—out of captivity and into blessing and promise. Today, we have forsaken God's truth that saved and blessed us. Nehemiah 9:35 is a perfect Scripture to describe our condition:

> *For they have not served You in their kingdom, or*
> *in the many good things that You gave them, or in*
> *the large and rich land which You set before them;*
> *nor did they turn from their wicked works.*

We live under a system of confusion that is becoming increasingly corrupt and evil. We have been taken captive in the natural and in the spiritual. And God in His great mercy and providence is so excited about His New Covenant Priesthood who is about to rise out of the culture of confusion that has produced compromising churches. We are in the midst of a great spiritual exodus which will be the impetus for an exodus in the natural. God is shaking the world so that His true Church will awaken out of their blindness and into the clarity and understanding of the truth of God's Word. A resolute, powerful, and compassionate army.

> *Nevertheless in Your great mercy You did not utterly consume them nor forsake them; For You are God, gracious and merciful* (Nehemiah 9:31).

Every biblical exodus involved a departing from slavery and into freedom. Today, we have been taken captive by a religion of cultural Christianity and its traditions. It is a form of godliness that denies power and functions through earthly patterns. As the Church has lost its true nature and identity as sons and daughters of light and power, the darkness has swept into our culture. The coming shaking will cause the Church to leave its four walls and country and discover her true self again.

In the exoduses of the Bible, God moved supernaturally to establish His people in worship, connecting them back to Himself in truth, friendship, and intimacy, moving heaven and earth on their behalf. This time the exodus is created through the remnant—the Christ ones—who have been crying out day and night, hungering for God's presence and will. As God told Reinhard Bonnke, "Your words in your mouth are as powerful as My words in My mouth." The earth is shaking under the words of a love-sick remnant who are releasing the sound of heaven, saying and singing, "Come Jesus, come."

Our coming exodus will involve similar components to Zerubbabel's exodus:

1. Shaking the systems of the earth
2. Outpouring of gold and silver to the saints (transfer of wealth)
3. A great awakening of our eyes and ears to access the excess of heaven's resources; saints moving in supernatural power and revealing the glory and nature of God.

The God of heaven and earth will arise through the shining ones who will awaken the Church and lead the way. God is releasing His government back to His Church to complete the work and ready the earth for His return. The true Church is who we are in our identity as Christ ones, not where we go on Sundays. The one message that God had during both exoduses and I believe He has for us today, "Do not fear, for I am with you." He lives in us and is for us taking our earth back. He gave it to us to rule and reign, and right now the devil is trespassing on our land.

Shaking the Systems of the Earth

Similar to Zerubbabel's exodus, the shaking will create a separation between the people of the culture of the world and the people of God. The shaking will take us from confusion (Babylon) and being led by our natural minds into real worship and being led by the Spirit of truth. Additionally, the shaking/separation was and is being initiated by the prophetic. Isaiah's prophecy to Cyrus created the spiritual impetus for the exodus.

Today, we see a reawakening of the prophetic all around the world and a growing and powerful prayer movement. Our prophetic intercession is creating the shaking in the earth that will cause the true Church to separate itself from the culture of confusion and live as children of God. In Matthew 24, Jesus warned that there will be natural disasters, failing economies, and foreign conflicts before His return. The world is experiencing these events now, and I believe they will increase in the coming days. However, God is using these very shakings to awaken His church, to set her apart from the world, and to empower her like never before. God is basically saying through His praying church to the culture of this age, "Let My people go." The church was called to be Kingdom change agents and culture setters.

We are commissioned to make the kingdom of this world look like the Kingdom of our God—not the other way around.

Gold and Silver—Transfer of Wealth

During the exoduses in the Bible, God used the process of shaking to free His people, but that in the shaking the people of the land would be required by Him to give the people of God their gold and silver. Today, He is shaking the earth:

> *For thus says the Lord of hosts: "Once more (it is a little while) I will shake heaven and earth, the*

sea and dry land; and I will shake all nations, and they shall come to the Desire of All Nations [Jesus] and I will fill this temple with glory," says the Lord of hosts. "The silver is Mine, and the gold is Mine," says the Lord of hosts. "The glory of this latter temple shall be greater than the former," says the Lord of hosts. "And in this place I will give peace [fullness],' says the Lord of hosts" (Haggai 2:6-9).

In the exodus of Moses, the people of the land gave the children of Israel their *gold, silver, and livestock,*

Now the children of Israel had done according to the word of Moses, and they had asked from the Egyptians articles of silver, articles of gold, and clothing. And the Lord had given the people favor in the sight of the Egyptians, so that they granted them what they requested. Thus they plundered the Egyptians (Exodus 12:35-36).

Remember in the exodus of Zerubbabel, twice the Lord moved, both on Cyrus and Darius (two Persian kings), to command the people of the land to give gold and silver to the children of Israel:

And all those who were around them encouraged them with articles of silver and gold, with goods and livestock, and with precious things, besides all that was willingly offered (Ezra 1:6).

Moreover I issue a decree as to what you shall do for the elders of these Jews, for the building of this house of God: Let the cost be paid at the king's expense from taxes on the region beyond the River; this is to be given immediately to these men, so that they are not hindered. And whatever they need—young bulls, rams, and lambs for the burnt offerings of the God of heaven, wheat, salt, wine, and oil, according to the request of the priests who are in Jerusalem— let it be given them day by day without fail, that they may offer sacrifices of sweet aroma to the God of heaven, and pray for the life of the king and his sons (Ezra 6:8-10).

As it was with every exodus, I see a great transfer of wealth coming to those who have the eyes to see and the ears to hear, who have faithfully sown into the Kingdom and followed the leadership of the Lord. They will be the Cyruses and Josephs of our day to provide for the coming awakening and harvest.

Out of Our Natural Minds and Into His

In Haggai 1:14, the Lord stirred up the spirit of Zerubbabel. The phrase "stirred up" means to awaken in their spiritual eyes. *As we wake up, we will see with our spiritual eyes and hear what the Spirit is saying.*

God is waking up His Church out of their confusion and into the truth. They will see and hear and know; then they will arise as a great army in unity. When the serpent of old came to Eve to tempt her, he didn't do it by tempting her outright. He challenged the Word of God (more of this in "The Plumb Line Cleanses the Prophetic" chapter). The sons of God are led by the Spirit, the Truth, of God. Currently, the Church is trying to win the lost by looking like and acting like the lost. We have been trying to live like worldly minded people of the earth. But the Bible says we are to set our minds on things above and live as citizens of heaven. John G. Lake, the great early-20th-century healing evangelist in the Pentecostal movement, said that if we eat of the earth instead of the bread of heaven, we will become like the earth with decay, death, and destruction. Our function is to bring heaven to the earth.

When God created the heavens and the earth, He created a system where heaven and earth functioned together as one unit. Since God existed before heaven and earth were created, the question Bob Hazlett asked in his book *Thinking Like Heaven*, is, "Why did God create heaven? It was the place He dwells to connect in friendship and love with His sons and daughters so He can co-rule and co-reign the earth with them." Hazlett also wrote, "Heaven was not intended as a 'retirement home' for deceased believers but as a place from which real life is lived. Adam was created to never die. So heaven was created so humans could interact with a living God!"

My prophetic friend Jamie Galloway said recently, "When God asked Adam, 'Where are you?' He wasn't asking him where he was on earth. He was asking, 'Where are you in heaven? Why have you left your heavenly dwelling place.'"

As we wake up, we begin to access the excess of heaven's resources and begin to live a Kingdom lifestyle—living *from* the Father's *heart and will* with demonstrations of greater works. This is the pattern Jesus spoke of and demonstrated. This shaking will produce a hardship for the earth dwellers, but it will be the greatest hour for the shining ones.

As our spiritual eyes are opened, we are leaving the patterns of earthly thinking where our un-renewed minds are transformed and become the source of our wisdom and knowledge. Paul writes to the Romans:

> *And do not be conformed to this world, but be transformed by the renewing of your mind, that you may prove what is that good and acceptable and perfect will of God* (Romans 12:2).

Paul very clearly understood the importance of a renewed mindset that is free from the pattern of thinking and words of the world and is connected to heaven so we can do what is the perfect will of God. Jesus told us that we would be set apart. Paul writes to the Ephesians about the benefits of the heaven and earth connection, being taught by Jesus through His words of truth that were spoken and written.

> *If indeed you have heard Him and have been taught by Him, as the truth is in Jesus: that you put off, concerning your former conduct, the old man which grows corrupt according to the deceitful lusts* [according to earthly patterns], *and be renewed in the spirit of your mind, and that you put on the new man which was created according to God, in true righteousness and holiness* (Ephesians 4:21-24).

Vision: Our Finest Hour

In 2015, I had a vision where I was taken to a room in heaven where the only one there was Jesus. It looked like a boardroom with a long table and many chairs. He told me to watch.

He had endless envelopes with the individual names of people on one side and the word FINEST HOUR on the other. He took one envelope and reached for a brick of *gold* and handed it to an angel that disappeared—like a marathon runner in a cartoon—to take it down to earth. He did this for a very long time. There was a line of angels waiting to receive their assignments. These envelopes were being given to those on the earth who have been marked as revealed in Ezekiel 9:4, *"and the Lord said to him, 'Go through the midst of the city, through the midst of Jerusalem, and put a mark on the foreheads of the men who sigh and cry over all the abominations that are done within it.'"*

Then I saw Jesus reach for something new. He began to add to certain envelopes a gold medal, like the ones given to Olympic athletes. They had red, white, and blue ribbons and were really beautiful. He said, "These are for the kings." I felt like they were being given to those who would lead many, the apostles. He handed the angels the envelopes named FINEST HOUR, the gold bars, and the gold medals and they flew to the earth. When He was finished, He turned, opened His mouth toward earth, and a loud trumpet sound came out. Then He became a great Lion and the trumpet sound became a great roar. Then the Lion leapt toward earth.

There are two groups in this vision. The first group is given resources to fund the coming awakening, and the second group are those who are being mantled as apostles to full authority to restore the earth. I see the days of Isaiah 60 and 61 coming on the saints of God who are being marked with His glory. *"Arise and shine; for your light has come! And the glory of the Lord has risen upon you. For behold, the darkness shall cover the earth, and deep darkness the people; But the Lord will arise over you, And His glory will be seen upon you."* and you shall rebuild, raise up, repair the desolations of generations.

As deep darkness covers the earth and there are signs in the sun, moon and stars, look up for your redemption draws nigh. Have courage and know, if God is for us, who can be against us? The God of heaven and earth has no difficulty moving on the spirit of the people of the land to do His pleasure of taking care of His people during times of the exoduses then and now. We can trust the Lord's leadership in this hour and have great hope for our FINEST HOUR.

6

THE FOUNDATION OF ZERUBBABEL'S TEMPLE

The hands of Zerubbabel have laid the foundation
of this temple; his hands shall finish it....
—ZECHARIAH 4:9

In ancient Israel, a master builder's work included laying the foundation and placing the capstone, the roof. He starts the work and also finishes the work. He leaves building the walls, rooms, windows, etc. to the workmen. He uses a plumb line or plummet stone to measure so that the foundation is true and rightly aligned. The plumb line would be hung from a wooden tripod-like structure from a string with a stone at the end. All the walls would be built in proportion to this plumb line to make sure that they were properly measured and built correctly. Remember, the plumb line is the Word of God, which is heaven's Truth.

Zerubbabel's temple is a pattern and shadow of the New Testament Church, which I will discuss in greater detail later, but keep that thought in mind as I describe this building process and how it relates to the prophetic symbolism in Ezra, Haggai, and Zechariah.

Zerubbabel was leading the radical, passionate remnant to lay the foundation of the temple. He was building a different kind of temple, one that was not made with human might or power but by the Holy Spirit. He understood that he was leading an exodus, transitioning the people of God out of confusion and into a new way of life and worship.

Ezra describes the entire community, *"...gathered together as one man to Jerusalem"* (Ezra 3:1). They arose and built the foundation and the altar of God for burnt offerings. This was a terrifying moment for the children of Israel. Many had grown up as slaves in Babylon. Here they had to build the altar of worship in the open for all of their Babylonian enemies in Jerusalem to see.

Two years after the foundation was laid, the Babylonians who remained in the land after the Persian conquest began to frustrate the building and discourage the people as they were working. They wrote a letter to the new king who had conquered Cyrus, and convinced him to command the temple building to cease. The work would not resume for another fourteen years. This graphic, I believe, is a picture of the past 1,800 years of church history.

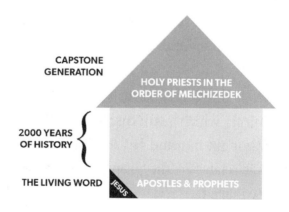

The New Covenant Temple

At Pentecost, the foundation of the human temple was laid when Jesus poured out His Spirit. The people began to gather their belongings and lay them at the apostles' feet. They gathered as a family, with Christ in them as their common union, communion. They began to build. Jesus the Master Builder laid the foundation of His temple on the apostles and prophets with Himself as its cornerstone.

> *We heard Him say, "I will destroy this temple made with hands, and within three days I will build another made without hands"* (Mark 14:58).
>
> *Now, therefore, you are no longer strangers and foreigners, but fellow citizens with the saints and members of the household of God, having been built on the foundation of the apostles and prophets, Jesus Christ Himself being the chief cornerstone, in whom the whole building, being fitted together, grows into a holy temple in the Lord, in whom you also are being built together for a dwelling place of God in the Spirit* (Ephesians 2:19-22).

After both Zerubbabel and Jesus' foundations were laid, the people of the land began to discourage, accuse, and frustrate the building. This is a picture of the past 1,800 years or more that the Church has grown, but not in its truest form. The church experienced resistance through persecution, doctrinal controversies, divisions, and control within the Church. Though Christianity spread throughout the centuries, the power that the apostles walked in, the plumb line of the voice of the Lord, and the New Covenant priesthood that Jesus and the apostles proclaimed became increasingly rare. Man began institutionalizing Christianity and establishing a religious form that took the place of the presence and power of God.

Jesus didn't go to the cross to create a religion that is a form of godliness that denies its power. He died to rebuild a new, living human temple that would house His Spirit, a new race, a holy priesthood. Through the years the Church has been but a shadow of its true self, for the most part because of the removal of the Word, the Spirit—hence, the prophetic— and the revelation of the temple of man releasing the power of God in the earth.

We have seen the Church regaining its identity over the past 500-plus years through the restoration of the saved-by-grace doctrine, Pentecostal revival, Latter Rain healing and miracle revival, the Father's love revival, prayer revival, and prophetic revival. All of these truths are preparing a vibrant and ready remnant to receive the finishing work of Christ in His last generation, the capstone generation.

There is another application of the revelation of laying the foundation, and the capstone is how it applies to our own personal temple. When we are born again and baptized in the Holy Spirit, our foundation is laid with access to heaven. Paul said that Jesus is faithful to finish what He started in us and He is the Author and Finisher of our faith:

> *Being confident of this, that he who began a good work in you will carry it on to completion until the day of Christ Jesus* (Philippians 1:6 NIV).

The people of the land will persecute, accuse, and frustrate you IF you are connected to heaven through His voice, prophesying, and have a disciplined and effective life in prayer through friendship and intimacy with Jesus. However, if you are joined to the religious culture and the system of this world, they will leave you alone.

> *See that you do not refuse Him who speaks. For if they did not escape who refused Him who spoke on earth, much more shall we not escape if we turn away from Him who speaks from heaven* (Hebrews 12:25).

Jesus, the Master Builder, laid the foundation through the first generation of His Church. If God is saying He wants Zerubbabel's temple rebuilt through multiple angelic messengers and signs, then I believe the generation has arrived where God is bringing the capstone, His finishing work before His return. Within these two defining generations was power and authority resulting in an incredible harvest of souls, the greatest harvest being the one that is coming.

7

REBUILDING THE TEMPLE THROUGH THE PROPHETS HAGGAI AND ZECHARIAH

The prophetic is the most valuable gift to the Body of Christ because it releases God's voice that will cause that generation to line up with His will. In 1999, the voice of the Lord spoke audibly to me, so I searched for answers. I ran to the institution of the church, but they told me that God doesn't talk anymore and concluded that I was hearing from a demon. I thank God that He led John and me to Sojourn Church with Terry and Susan Moore who discipled us in the full gospel and helped us to grow in the gifts of the Holy Spirit.

Over the past twenty years, we have seen a restoration of the prophetic ministry to the Church around the world. When you see an increase in the prophetic, you can be sure that God is doing something big. Every time God transitioned His people, He did it through His agents of change, the prophets. I believe this increase in the prophetic is in direct response to the exploding prayer movement worldwide. When there is prayer in the Body of Christ, the prophetic follows. When the Church gives herself to hearing God's voice in prayer, the result is the prophetic.

The rising tide of the prophetic that is sweeping the earth today has initiated the shift from religious activities of the Church to preparing the Body of Christ for the transition into their identity as a Kingdom of priests. For centuries, we have relied on human traditions to build the Church, but God is teaching us once again to operate in His Kingdom, in the powers of the age to come, just as the apostles did.

At Pentecost, God was restoring His voice back to the Church. I believe Pentecost was but a tithe of what we can expect in the coming days. The primary sign of the outpouring of the Holy Spirit would be an explosion of the prophetic ministry. *All* would prophesy, *all* would hear the voice of the Lord:

> *And it shall come to pass in the last days, says God, that I will pour out of My Spirit on all flesh; your sons and your daughters shall prophesy, your young men shall see visions, your old men shall dream dreams. And on My menservants and on My maidservants I will pour out My Spirit in those days; and they shall prophesy* (Acts 2:17-18).

John the Baptist was the greatest prophet who ever lived under the Old Covenant order, but Jesus said that even the least in the Kingdom of heaven would be greater than he is (Matthew 11:11). Because of the outpouring of the Holy Spirit, even the least in the Kingdom would prophesy, bringing His truth from heaven to earth.

Sadly, many in the Church today have been resistant to the prophetic, even calling it demonic. We are entering a time when the Lord will no longer tolerate this. I will boldly and confidently say that churches that continue to reject the voice of the Lord through the prophetic will begin to fade away. But churches that embrace it, teach about it, and equip the saints to operate in it will arise. They will be the ones who truly build on the foundation that Jesus laid in the first-century Church. They will be the ones who establish His people as *"a dwelling place of God in the Spirit"* (Ephesians 2:22) who release the voice of the Lord to the earth.

As God used Haggai and Zechariah to re-initiate the work of Zerubbabel's temple, so once again He is using the prophetic to awaken His people to begin to rebuild according to heaven's blueprint, not an earthly model or a church franchise. God used an angel to speak to Zechariah about the coming human temple and the priesthood that will operate in it. God uses symbols through these visions to define the role of Zerubbabel as a king in Zechariah 4 and define the role of Joshua, a priest in Zechariah 3. I introduce these Scriptures to bring understanding of the meaning of the symbols and my interpretation. Then I introduce Haggai's prophetic promises and blessings that this kind of New Testament priest will operate under and in.

Zerubbabel's function as a king described in Zechariah 4 and Joshua's function as a priest in Zechariah 3 serve as prophetic symbols of the end-time apostolic church operating as both priests and kings. From God's point of view, the task of rebuilding this temple in which the priest and king were engaged was the greatest and most important thing in the world because it formed the center of His governmental authority and the motive of His providential dealings on the earth. God's establishment of this temple with its kingly and priestly dimensions would serve as the centerpiece of His governmental system for releasing heaven on earth.

The question today remains, as it did in the first-century Church: can people be ruled *internally* by the Spirit of God, functioning as king-priests, or do they need to be *outwardly* ruled by religion and rules? If it's not the first, then it will be the second. The apostles functioned as king-priests who were governed internally by the Spirit, but sadly, over time, religion and rules took over and ruled humankind outwardly. Behavior was managed, rules were enforced, but hearts were not transformed. There was a form of godliness, but no power.

But Zechariah's vision shows us that the foundation of this internal rule of God's Spirit that the apostles operated in will return with the capstone, the end-time generation. Once again, humankind will learn to be governed not *outwardly* as *slaves* by human traditions and earthly wisdom but *internally* as *sons and daughters* by the Spirit of the Lord.

> *For those who are led by the Spirit of God are the children of God* (Romans 8:14 NIV).

If our generation will embrace this inward government by the Spirit, then a double portion of grace will be given to us, and no obstacle will stand before us in experiencing the fullness of Christ in joy, love, hope, and power as we advance His Kingdom on earth. This is where the fun and freedom begins.

Now for Zechariah's vision. I'll start with Zechariah 4 and the kingly role since this chapter also describes the temple—with the foundation and capstone—and the ministry of *both* priest and king in the temple. Then we'll look at Zechariah 3 to look more closely at our priestly role.

Zechariah 4

Zechariah 4 is a key Scripture for the awakening of the Church that will initiate the end-time harvest. I hope that the message of Zechariah 4 will stir up your spirit to build according to His blueprint as an individual and corporate body.

Zechariah chapter 4 has three parts:

- Part 1 (verses 1-5): The Vision
- Part 2 (verses 6-10): The Message
- Part 3 (verses 11-14): The Interpretation

Part 1: The Vision

1-3 Now the angel who talked with me came back and wakened me, as a man who is wakened out of his sleep. And he said to me, "What do you see?" So I said, "I am looking, and there is a lampstand of solid gold with a bowl on top of it, and on the stand seven lamps with seven pipes to the seven lamps. Two olive trees are by it, one at the right of the bowl and the other at its left."

So an angel *awakens* Zechariah from his sleep to show him a vision with three things: 1) a *lampstand*—that represents us as the Church or living temple giving the light to the world—of solid gold with *seven torches* and *seven pipes* that feed into the seven torches; 2) a *bowl* on top of the lampstand; and 3) *two olive trees* on either side of the bowl. Keep in mind this theme of awakening. So here is the vision, but what is its significance?

Part 2: *The Message*

> *6–7 So he answered and said to me: "This is the word of the Lord to Zerubbabel: 'Not by might nor by power, but by My Spirit,' says the Lord of hosts. 'Who are you, O great mountain? Before Zerubbabel you shall become a plain! And he shall bring forth the capstone with shouts of "Grace, grace to it!"'*
>
> *8-10 Moreover the word of the Lord came to me, saying: "The hands of Zerubbabel have laid the foundation of this temple; his hands shall also finish it. Then you will know that the Lord of hosts has sent Me to you. For who has despised the day of small things? For these seven rejoice to see the plumb line in the hand of Zerubbabel. They are the eyes of the Lord, which scan to and fro throughout the whole earth."*

The key message here is: this temple will be completed by and functioning in the power of the Spirit of the Lord, not human power or wisdom. The foundation is laid and the capstone will be placed. No obstacle will hinder the completion and ministry of the temple because God is pouring out a double portion of grace. It will start small, but when it is rightly aligned with heaven's word—the plumb line—it will operate in the power of the seven spirits of God—the seven eyes and the seven torches—and its influence will spread around the entire earth. The Lord continues to show Zechariah the significance of the two olive trees.

Part 3: The Interpretation

> 11–14 *Then I answered and said to him, "What are these two olive trees—at the right of the lampstand and at its left?" And I further answered and said to him, "What are these two olive branches that drip into the receptacles of the two gold pipes from which the golden oil drains?"*
>
> *Then he answered me and said, "Do you not know what these are?" And I said, "No, my lord."*
>
> *So he said, "These are the two anointed ones, who stand beside the Lord of the whole earth."*

The last verse is key. The two olive trees that pour out golden oil into the bowl are *"the two anointed ones* [Christ ones], *who stand beside the Lord of the earth."* So the olive trees are roles, *anointed people* who stand in the presence of God and whose ministry fuels the function of the new temple. There is a lot going on here, so I want to break down the symbols and talk about how each one applies to the New Covenant temple made not of stones but of people (1 Peter 2:5).

Some may say that Zechariah's vision applies only to the temple that Zerubbabel built; but as we look at each symbol, we find some elements that weren't fulfilled in Zerubbabel's temple.

In fact, Zerubbabel's temple was the temple that rejected Jesus, whose veil was torn and altar split in two when Jesus died on the cross.

There have only been two temples built in Israel: Solomon's and Zerubbabel's. The temple in the New Testament is called Herod's temple because he renovated and expanded the original version of Zerubbabel's temple. But that temple was not torn down until after the Romans destroyed it in AD 70. So as we look at each of the symbols in this vision of Zechariah 4, we see that there is a temple yet to come about which Zechariah was prophesying. There are four symbols in this prophecy that tell of a coming supernatural human temple whose Master Builder is Jesus Christ:

1. The candlestick changed its functionality from that of the first temple.

Solomon's temple: If you look at the candlestick or Menorah from Solomon's temple (Diagram 1), you will see that it is designed per the instructions given to Moses on the mountain (Exodus 25:31-40).

The golden candlestick or lampstand was made for the purpose of keeping light in the temple day and night. It represented Jesus as the Light of the world. The priests in the order of Zadok and Aaron were responsible for keeping oil in its bowels, located at the top of each candlestick. The oil was supplied through the people, sacrificially giving the priests freshly pressed olive oil. The oil was coming from *the might and power of man*, daily crushing the olives.

2. Two olive branches/trees—new priesthood of Jesus.

> *And I further answered and said to him, "What are these two olive branches that drip into the receptacles of the two gold pipes from which the golden oil drains?" Then he answered me and said, "Do you not know what these are?" And I said, "No, my lord." So he said, "These are the two anointed ones, who stand beside the Lord of the whole earth"* (Zechariah 4:12-14).

The candlestick of Zerubbabel's temple that Zechariah sees in this vision, though, was crafted differently and the oil came from a different source. The angel of the Lord introduced a new type of candlestick that was filled with the oil that resulted from intimacy and obedience, not sacrifice. *This* oil spontaneously flowed through *the might and power of the Holy Spirit* and did not require toil and labor. Obedience, not sacrifice.

The golden candlestick that Zechariah saw is filled with oil that poured from the branches of these two olive trees, filling the bowl and then assimilating the oil into the seven candlesticks. Again, there is a change in the way the oil is achieved. It no longer comes from the external work of sacrifice of the Old Testament priesthood but through grace—an internal reality of the Christ in us that spontaneously produces oil.

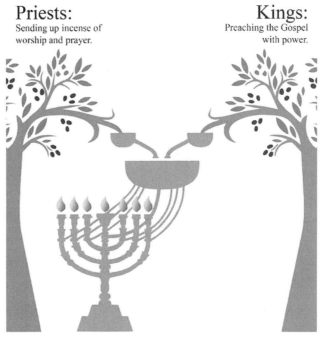

Priests:
Sending up incense of
worship and prayer.

Kings:
Preaching the Gospel
with power.

The Golden Lampstand
Zechariah 4

The two olive branches/trees that are spontaneously producing oil are the two offices of the priest and king, which make up the governmental authority of God on earth. I am focusing on the kingly branch in this section of Zechariah 4 and will highlight the priestly branch later in Zechariah 3. The two branches together form God's chosen government. A good comparison are branches of government in the United States—Legislative, Judicial, and Executive— which make up the operations of the country. Each one functions differently but completes the whole government as they work together.

Dream: 2008

In a dream, I saw these two olive trees and written on the one on the left was PRIEST and on the one on the right, KING.

Joshua was the high priest (Zechariah 3) who partnered with Zerubbabel in rebuilding the temple. As already stated, Zerubbabel was in the line of David and the heir apparent to the throne of David. So the roles of Joshua and Zerubbabel as the anointed ones were priest and king, respectively.

Let's look at the Hebrew meaning of the *anointed ones.* The word *anointed* is *yitshav*: oil that produces light. The word *ones* is *ben* in Hebrew: sons (a builder of the family name). So the *anointed ones* means *sons of oil.* Jesus, the Son of God, was given the title "Christ," which means the *Anointed One, Son of Oil,* or *Son of Light.* So when the Lord says to Zechariah that these *two olive branches* are the *anointed ones,* He is saying that they are sons of oil, sons of light, or the *Christ ones.* These are the ones who would come through the death and resurrection of Christ who ransomed us and seated us in heavenly places of authority.

Jesus as the firstborn of many is the chief Christ, or Anointed One. But He poured out the golden oil of His Spirit to dwell in us and make us into many "christs," anointed ones, who would function as kings and priests in His living temple.

Notice also that the two anointed ones of Zechariah 4 are those who "stand beside the Lord of the whole earth." The kingly and priestly offices receive their life and power from standing in the presence of the Lord. As we abide in the presence of the Lord as priests, we can function in His power and authority as kings.

I believe these are the messages of Revelation 10 being opened for the equipping of the saints to help them in becoming the rebuilt temple of Christ. Christ is coming to take up habitation in its fullness in His temple in these last days.

This anointing flows as we function in our roles and produces a double portion of grace—power and anointing. As we pray as priests, oil is created by the power of the Holy Spirit; and as we release the words and actions of heaven as kings, another portion of oil is released by the power of the Holy Spirit. So there is a portion of *grace* that comes from standing before the Lord as a *priest* and another portion of *grace* that comes from standing before the Lord as a *king*. These two together are the grace—grace anointing that creates the lifestyle of "the gates of hell will not prevail against you" (Matthew 16:18) and "you will heal the sick, raise the dead and cast out demons" (Matthew 10:8). As the church learns to operate as priests and kings, the kingdom of darkness will not be able to stand. The Kingdom of heaven will advance with power and authority.

Dream: I was given a doorframe that had two doors in it. They were not side by side but one was in front of the other in the doorframe. I was told that I was being given double doors. Which reminded me of what Isaiah 45 wrote about Cyrus as he was commanded to rebuild Zerubbabel's temple:

...To Cyrus, whose right hand I have held—to subdue nations before him and loose the armor of kings, to open before him the double doors, so that the gates will not be shut (Isaiah 45:1).

3. The plumb line has fallen.

Zerubbabel could only build the temple properly with the plumb line in his hands. Remember, the plumb line is what properly levels the foundation and aligns the building accordingly. The plumb line here symbolizes *the Truth of God's Word* that comes from heaven to earth. This is how the apostles and prophets of the first-century Church built the New Covenant temple. They were filled with the Spirit at Pentecost and built according to His might and power, His wisdom and leading— not the teaching and traditions of men.

This is the kingly role that I mentioned when talking about the two olive trees. The kingly role that Zechariah saw are those who release what is in heaven to earth. What's important to remember, however, is that the plumb line, the truth, falls because of the activity and role of the priests. The priests hear and see, the kings declare and act. The kings are aligned by declaring and doing only what they see and hear from heaven. Later I will address this more in practical terms as to how it applies in our lives. Jesus our King-Priest, lived and built this way. He is the Forerunner and Model of the kingly priesthood He came to establish. Jesus said:

"...I do nothing of Myself; but as My Father taught Me, I speak these things. And He who sent Me is with Me. The Father has not left Me alone, for I

always do those things that please Him" (John 8:28-29).

The plumb line fell into Zerubbabel's hands and the seven eyes—the seven spirits of God—rejoiced. Why did they rejoice? Because now that the plumb line was released, the temple could be rebuilt properly.

This is important to the Lord as He has sent several angels and He Himself appeared to announce "the plumb line is now in the hands of Zerubbabel." Therefore, I have dedicated an entire chapter to what I believe is revelation for the Church today; the purpose of the plumb line and how to access and apply it to prosper and overcome in our lives and to advance Christ's Kingdom on earth.

In the first church with the apostles, the plumb line was readily available, leading them into all truth and laying the foundation of the faith. However, in many churches, pastors offer their people heretical teaching that God doesn't speak anymore. The plumb line is absent, which keeps their people in the confused state of darkness, earthly living and reasoning, religious practices, witchcraft (control and manipulation), and wilderness living. Today, we see a re-emergence of the plumb line with the increase of the apostles and prophets functioning in faith, hearing, seeing, and delivering the truth from heaven with power to reform and transform the Church and the earth.

4. The foundation and the capstone were symbolic of two ages of time.

Christ laid the foundation of the New Covenant temple made of living stones—you and me—through grace, grace on the day of Pentecost when He poured out His Spirit. The plumb line of truth from heaven to earth was in His hands to build. Jesus as the Chief Cornerstone initiated the work of the New Covenant temple. He was the first stone of many that were laid and are being laid. Then He laid the foundation through the apostles and prophets, who had the plumb line of His Word. They heard from heaven and built accordingly.

However, shortly after the building began, false teachers and false prophets brought frustration, confusion, accusation, and discouragement. The Church stopped building according to the plumb line—the truth or Word—of the Spirit and began incorporating human traditions and teachings.

Man-made religion replaced the truth of the "new man" and the Church for the most part was powerless for almost 2,000 years. The truth of the new man is the new race of sons and daughters who are born again, baptized in the Holy Spirit and fire, with Christ in them. They are primarily people of prayer who understand how to function in prayer effectively and see the fulfillment of those prayers in the earth. Jesus died and rose again so that He could dwell inside humanity through the baptism of the Holy Spirit and fire. He wanted a temple of men and women full of His Spirit who would build by *His* might and power, not by their own.

But once again in our generation, God has broken in with the apostolic and prophetic to "stir up" the Church like Haggai and Zechariah to begin building again in the same way as in the beginning. There is a remnant that has found the ancient ways of God and of the original builders and is beginning to tap into the plumb line from heaven to earth within them.

Once again, as the angels announced, the plumb line is in the hand of Zerubbabel, meaning the completion of the temple has begun.

This plumb line is once again in the hand of Jesus through His sons and daughters. They are the capstone, the last generation and the finishing work of Christ-men and Christ-women on the earth taking the Kingdom with them wherever they go and in whatever they do. No matter which mountain they are called to—the Church, media, science, business, education, family, or entertainment—this generation of capstone people will invade these areas.

Zechariah 3: The Cleansing of God's Priesthood

I have focused more on the role of Zerubbabel than Joshua, but both have equally important roles. The angel of the Lord appears to both. However, He first speaks to Joshua about the condition and transformation of the priesthood, before he addresses the role of the king with Zerubbabel. I love how the Lord is invested in the sanctification of the priest. He is the One who does the cleansing and silences the accuser.

Zechariah sees Joshua the high priest standing before the Lord in filthy garments. Satan accuses Joshua but the Lord rebukes the accuser and tells those surrounding Joshua, "Take away the filthy garments from him." The Lord was removing Joshua's iniquity so He could clothe him with "rich robes" of righteousness. Not only was He giving Joshua clean garments, but also a clean turban. God was in essence saying, "I want to sanctify My priests through the washing of the Word, through renewing their minds."

> *...as Christ also loved the church and gave Himself
> for her, that He might sanctify and cleanse her
> with the washing of water by the word, that He
> might present her to Himself a glorious church, not
> having spot or wrinkle or any such thing, but that
> she should be holy and without blemish* (Ephesians
> 5:25-27).

> *And do not be conformed to this world, but be trans-
> formed by the renewing of your mind, that you may
> prove what is that good and acceptable and perfect
> will of God* (Romans 12:2).

Righteousness is living in the Kingdom and living through His ways in the Kingdom. Kingdom living is right living because it is living according to the words of our King Jesus Christ. Through the cleansing of Joshua's mind and the actions of his life, he is rightly aligned to take his position of authority. When his mind and heart are cleaned up, heaven's words can rightly filter through him without being corrupted, manipulated, or misunderstood.

The Lord gave a promise to Joshua that if he would walk in the ways of the Lord (the ways of the Kingdom) and obey His commands (His Word), then He would judge in the house of the Lord, take charge in His courts, and walk among those who stand before the Lord (Zechariah 3:7). In other words, Joshua, as a holy priest, will step into a supernatural realm of wisdom, authority, and intimacy with God.

There are many in the church today who have *"defiled their garments"* (Revelation 3:4) by forsaking the Word of the Lord. We have allowed the wisdom and culture of the world to dictate how we operate. But Jesus is cleansing His Church from a filthy turban of worldly thinking and filthy garments of worldly living. He is setting her apart as a holy priesthood whose thoughts, words, and actions are in accordance with His Word, which is truth.

> *Sanctify them by Your truth. Your word is truth* (John 17:17).

Zechariah's visions of Zerubbabel and Joshua prophesy of a coming temple—a human temple built by Jesus, our King-Priest—and His New Covenant priesthood. This priesthood will be a holy priesthood that functions both as priests and kings. They will have the mind and heart of God, and they will be in full alignment with His Word.

What is important to note is that the kingly role of Zerubbabel described in Zechariah 4 could not happen until the priestly role of Joshua was sanctified and set in place in Zechariah 3. Over the past twenty years or so, the worldwide prayer movement has been spreading rapidly. God has been using the International House of Prayer in Kansas City to call His Church back to David's one desire of gazing at the beauty of the Lord and inquiring in His temple (Psalm 27:4) and to Mary of Bethany's lifestyle of sitting at the feet of Jesus and hearing His Word (Luke 10:39). The prayer movement has also trumpeted a strong message of holiness of heart.

We have been in a Zechariah 3 moment as God has once again been establishing His Church in the priestly role of Joshua as a house of prayer with a holy priesthood. Now we are stepping into Zechariah 4 in the kingly role of Zerubbabel where we will also begin to operate in true Kingdom authority with a double portion of grace. We will not leave the priestly role as we learn to operate in this kingly role—we will function in both.

Haggai: Consider Your Ways

We have heard from the prophet Zechariah about our function and roles of the priest and king as the New Covenant priesthood; however, there are also prophetic promises for this generation through the prophet Haggai. As we function in the roles of this priesthood and are building according to His blueprint, the blessings from Haggai will be ours. The beauty of Haggai's prophecy is its application to the first and last generation.

When Zerubbabel the governor of Judah, Joshua the high priest, and the remnant of the people were commanded by the Persian government to cease the building of the temple, they turned to building their own houses for fourteen years. But then the Lord stirred up His Spirit in the prophets Haggai and Zechariah so they would awaken His people to begin rebuilding and bring the completion, the capstone, of His temple.

God has broken into our generation today with the restoration of the prophetic, not just with a super prophet here or there. He has distributed the prophetic gift throughout the Body of Christ. When multiple angelic messengers say, *"The plumb line is NOW in the hand of Zerubbabel,"* we can surmise that the prophetic words of Zechariah and Haggai are for us, the capstone generation, trumpeting His coming finished work. He spoke audibly to me that Zerubbabel's temple was going to be "rebuilt," which means He is awakening us to be His reformers and prepare for His coming return. He is rebuilding His people today into a living temple that ministers to the Lord as priests and operates in the anointing of the Holy Spirit as kings to bring heaven to earth. He is maturing us as sons and daughters who are led by the Spirit and built up into the unity of the faith.

I believe we are in the season of this rebuilding where God will supernaturally be calling His people to come out of "Babylon," to come out of confusion, where they have been building things made of wood, hay, and stubble (1 Corinthians 3:12). The scales are falling off our eyes to see the truth of who we are in Christ and who Christ is in us. There is grace to leave the wisdom and culture of this age and to walk in the wisdom and culture of the Kingdom.

Haggai prophesied not only to Zerubbabel, but to the church's present condition, admonishing us to stop building according to the "Babylonian way," according to human wisdom and human ways that leads to little victory or power—and to begin building according to God's wisdom and God's ways.

> Now therefore, thus says the Lord of hosts, "Consider your ways! You have sown much, and bring in little; you eat, but do not have enough; you drink, but you are not filled with drink; you clothe yourselves, but no one is warm; and he who earns wages, earns wages to put into a bag with holes." Thus says the Lord of hosts: "Consider your ways!" (Haggai 1:5-7)

"Go up to the mountains and bring wood and build the temple, that I may take pleasure in it and be glorified," says the Lord. "You looked for much, but indeed it came to little; and when you brought it home, I blew it away. Why?" says the Lord of hosts. "Because of My house that is in ruins, while every one of you runs to his own house. Therefore, the heavens above you withhold the dew, and the earth withholds its fruit. For I called for a drought on the land and the mountains, on the grain and the new wine and the oil, on whatever the ground brings forth, on men and livestock, and on all the labor of your hands" (Haggai 1:8-11).

Haggai is speaking to the remnant about *how* they are building not what they are building. He says several times, *consider your ways.* The people of Israel were building their own houses according to their own ways, and they did not understand why they were bearing no fruit. God wanted them to prosper and bear good fruit, but they would have to return to building God's house according to *God's ways.* Then they would truly prosper.

God was telling them that His living temples are designed to facilitate His Kingdom through a heaven-to-earth system not an earth-to-earth system. He is once again telling us that what we eat, drink, reap, and earn must come from heaven, not earth. From His ways, not our ways. From His strategies and methodologies, not our own.

God is calling His Church today to take a close look at how we are building and the fruit we are bearing. How are we building our lives, our churches, our families, and our businesses? As James tells us, when we build our lives according to earthly wisdom, according to our own ways and with selfish ambition, we bear the fruit of disorder, confusion, and wickedness.

> But if you harbor bitter envy and selfish ambition in your hearts, do not boast about it or deny the truth. Such "wisdom" does not come down from heaven but is earthly, unspiritual, demonic. For where you have envy and selfish ambition, there you find disorder and every evil practice (James 3:14-16 NIV).

We are trying to reign as kings on the earth, we are trying to prosper, but we are doing it our way, not God's. This is the Babylonian system out of which God is calling His people today. When we operate in our own ways, strategies, and methodologies, we are operating in lawlessness. What we are building in this Babylonian way will not stand in the current shaking, and it will burn up before the Judgment Seat of Christ.

> Now if anyone builds on this foundation with gold, silver, precious stones, wood, hay, straw, each one's work will become clear; for the Day will declare it, because it will be revealed by fire; and the fire will test each one's work, of what sort it is. If anyone's work which he has built on it endures, he will receive a reward. If anyone's work is burned, he will suffer loss; but he himself will be saved, yet so as through fire (1 Corinthians 3:12-15).

Only when we "consider our ways" and return to building according to God's ways—to heavenly wisdom—can we bear the good fruits of righteousness and peace.

> *But the wisdom that comes from heaven is first of all pure; then peace-loving, considerate, submissive, full of mercy and good fruit, impartial and sincere. Peacemakers who sow in peace reap a harvest of righteousness* (James 3:17-18 NIV).

As Jesus says in Matthew 6:25,33:

> *Therefore I say to you, do not worry about your life, what you will eat or what you will drink; nor about your body, what you will put on. Is not life more than food and the body more than clothing? ...But seek first the kingdom of God and His righteousness, and all these things shall be added to you.*

The people of Israel in Haggai's day were seeking first their own kingdoms, their own needs, and their own ambitions. They were building according to their own wisdom, not God's. They were trying to reign in the earth as kings, but they were forsaking their role as priests who stand in the presence of the Lord to receive wisdom from heaven on how to build and prosper. But once the word of the Lord came through Haggai, the people "feared the presence of the Lord." Then the Lord stirred up the spirit of Zerubbabel, Joshua, and the remnant of the people, and they turned back to building according to God's ways.

Have you ever had your spirit stirred? Once the prophetic is released, it causes the eyes of our hearts to open and our spirits to be stirred to give witness to and obey the voice of the Lord to do the works of the Kingdom. The Lord is stirring up His people today to "consider our ways," to consider how we are building. He is saying, "Stop seeking first your own ambitions, your own desires—and seek first the Kingdom of God and My righteousness. Let My wisdom and My ways govern how you spend your time, your money, and your energy." This means we must learn to stand in the presence of the Lord as priests *first*. This is how we receive the wisdom from heaven, the ways of God. We get our minds renewed by God's presence and God's Word. Then we can hear clearly. He speaks to us, and He tells us how to build. From that place we can prosper as kings and reign in the earth with Him. This is the New Testament priesthood, and this is the only way that the Church will enjoy the blessings of the Kingdom.

Haggai's Prophetic Promises to the Last Generation

Haggai prophesied three promises of blessing to those who will "consider their ways" and "Rebuild God's temple:" 1) the glory of God; 2) the gold and the silver; and 3) the signet ring of authority. While Haggai was speaking to his own generation in the natural, these prophetic promises were never fulfilled in the physical temple of his day. God is declaring these same promises to the last generation on the earth before the return of Jesus. These promises are available to those who function in this system of the New Testament priesthood and build the true spiritual temple: God-within believers.

1. God's glory will be poured out in His children.

> *For thus says the Lord of hosts: "Once more I will shake heaven and earth, the sea and dry land; and I will shake all nations, and they shall come to the Desire of All Nations, and I will fill this temple with glory," says the Lord of hosts. "The silver is Mine, and the gold is Mine," says the Lord of hosts. "The glory of this latter temple shall be greater than the former," says the Lord of hosts. "And in this place I will give peace," says the Lord of hosts* (Haggai 2:6-9).

Zerubbabel's physical temple never contained the glory of the Lord. In fact, the Ark of the Covenant, where the Lord's glory dwelt, disappeared at the time of the Babylonian captivity, so the presence of the Lord was absent. However, the temple He was speaking of was the temple I have already referred to in Hebrews 9:11, the temple not made of hands but a human temple created by God where the habitation of His glory dwells. Haggai prophecies that this is about the former and latter generation of *human temples* and points out that the last or latter generation will be greater in power, glory and peace. He will increase in us from glory to glory. As we function in the roles of priest *and* king, Christ is fully resident within us.

> *Father, I desire that they also whom You gave Me may be with Me where I am, that they may behold My glory which You have given Me; for You loved Me before the foundation of the world* (John 17:24).

To them God willed to make known what are the riches of the glory of this mystery among the Gentiles: which is Christ in you, the hope of glory (Colossians 1:27).

For I consider that the sufferings of this present time are not worthy to be compared with the glory which shall be revealed in us (Romans 8:18).

2. Silver and gold will be poured out.

It is interesting how Haggai is prophesying about the glory and he throws a verse in about silver and gold. If you break down the whole book of Haggai, you will see that there are conditions to its promises. He presents an *if* you do this, *then* you will get this scenario. If you stop building your lives according to the world system (the Babylonian system of confusion) and operate in the Kingdom system of the priest-king model, then silver and gold are going to be poured out. It is the wealth of the wicked that has been stored up for the righteous that will be distributed for the harvest. (I share some testimonies about how to apply and realize this in a later chapter.)

The Lord goes on to say through Haggai,

"And I will shake all nations, and they shall come to the Desire of All Nations, and I will fill this temple with glory," says the Lord of hosts. "The silver is Mine, and the gold is Mine," says the Lord of hosts (Haggai 2:7-8).

As the glory is poured out, it creates a shaking that creates alignment with His Word, producing fruitfulness and prosperity in His priesthood. And next you will see the signet ring, which is additional evidence of this abundance.

3. I will make you a signet ring.

In Scripture, God uses the symbol of a signet ring to represent the signature or name of the King. It is His complete authority, confidence of a person's loyalty, alignment, and assignment. He gives it to men and women who have His mind, His will, and His Word. In Haggai, he communicates this differently by saying that He is going to *make* you His signet ring. As you function in this role as priest-king, you are going to be made into His image and given His authority. This is the Galatians 2:20 maturing of the sons and daughters, "It is no longer I who lives but Christ who lives in me...."

A great comparison is the signet ring given to Joseph by Pharaoh. After Joseph interpreted his dream and gave wise counsel regarding the preparation for famine, Pharaoh told Joseph:

> *"You shall be over my house and all my people shall be ruled according to your word; only in regard to the throne will I be greater than you." ...Then Pharaoh took his signet ring off his hand and put it on Joseph's hand...* (Genesis 41:40,42).

This is an incredible promise of complete authority that we, the capstone generation, will be living and functioning in.

As we operate in the priest-king priesthood: 1) God will pour out His *glory* in our temple; 2) we will become His signature or *complete authority* in the earth; and 3) we will access even the *wealth of the nations* to distribute and build, or prepare, for His coming Kingdom harvest. Now let's talk about what the New Testament says about this priesthood.

REVELATION — ACCESS HEAVEN, TRANSFORM EARTH

8

THE MELCHIZEDEK PRIESTHOOD OF THE NEW TEMPLE

Zerubbabel's temple is a prophetic symbol of the living temple of God in humankind. The new priesthood of this living temple will operate in the order of Melchizedek as kings and priests.

Heaven's Perspective

In Revelation chapter 5, a remarkable scene unfolds as John the beloved sees the activity of heaven and the One who sits on the throne in all His splendor. Arrayed in dazzling colors, He is surrounded with multitudes of mighty angelic beings, twenty-four elders on thrones with crowns and white robes, four living creatures full of eyes all over their heavenly bodies, and seven blazing flames of fire. In His right hand, He holds a scroll written on two sides and it is sealed with seven seals.

A strong angel cries out, "Who is worthy to take the scroll and break its seals?" And no one in heaven, earth, or under the earth was found. All of a sudden, in the midst of the throne, the four living creatures, and the twenty-four elders, appears a Lamb standing as though it had been slain. He takes the scroll from the right hand of Him who is seated on the throne. When

He takes the scroll, jubilee breaks out in heaven. I believe the scroll is the legal document of ownership of the heavens and the earth and all that is in it. It is written on two sides, heaven and earth. Now both are under the leadership of the Lion of the tribe of Judah. The twenty-four elders fall down before Him, each holding golden bowls filled with incense, which are the prayers of the saints.

Then it happened. All of heaven began to sing "a new song." The new song is sung in Revelation 5:9-10:

> *You are worthy to take the scroll, and to open its seals; for You were slain, and have redeemed us to God by Your blood out of every tribe and tongue and people and nation, and have made us kings and priests to our God; and we shall reign on the earth.*

The new song is heaven's perspective and summation of what transpired at the cross. I believe this is the song of the capstone generation. Jesus has ascended into heaven at the Father's right hand. He has poured out His Spirit in us, laying the foundation of His new, living temple. A new song in heaven will break out. This new song will release a great revelation of the worthiness of Christ and authority that the Church has as kings and priests. The new song tells us:

- Why is Jesus worthy to open the scroll? *Because of His blood.*
- Who did He do this for? Every tribe, tongue, people, and nation.

- What did He accomplish in this redemption? *Made us kings* and *priests to our God.*

- Why does He make us kings and priests? So we can rule and reign (governmental authority).

- Where will humans reign? *On the earth.*

Jesus is worthy to take dominion of the entire earth because of His sacrifice on the cross. By His blood, He redeemed people from every tribe, people, nation, and language back to God. But He did something else, too. *He made us kings and priests* who will rule and reign with him *forever.* This has the same meaning as "I will make you like a signet ring" prophesied by the prophet Haggai. Notice where it says we will reign—*on the earth.* Though we are seated in Christ in the heavenly places (Ephesians 2:6), we reign on the earth. We release the power and authority of Christ who is seated in heaven *to the earth.* This is what Zechariah prophesied: a living temple with a priesthood that functions as kings and priests.

The book of Revelation reveals to us God's ultimate purpose, or result, of our redemption—to make us kings and priests who reign with Him forever. But what does this look like? How do we live as priests and kings? The book of Hebrews offers us great insight.

Introducing the New Priesthood of Melchizedek

The writer of Hebrews introduces us to the new temple that is not made with hands. It tells us about the priesthood of Jesus in the order of Melchizedek. I realize you just read several chapters about Zerubbabel's temple and now I am introducing another character from the Bible with an equally long name. At least the Holy Spirit didn't ask me to write a book on one of Isaiah's sons: Maher-Shalal-Hash-Baz.

> *But Christ came as High Priest of the good things to come, with the greater and more perfect tabernacle not made with hands, that is, not of this creation* (Hebrews 9:11).

Jesus demonstrated the new management system, that of an interior life of governmental rule instead of an exterior life of activities and traditions. He told us in Hebrews that the law has now gone within humans, meaning God's Word would not just govern our external behavior, but it will create in us the very internal likeness of Himself. This oneness with the Godhead will create His same outward expressions—power, love, miracles. This is the new order of priesthood Jesus died to recreate.

The writer of Hebrews tells us to move beyond the elementary principles of repentance from dead works and faith toward God, of the doctrine of baptisms, of laying on of hands, of resurrection of the dead, and eternal judgment—and go on to perfection, into a life of the new priesthood in the order of Melchizedek, who was both a king and priest:

> *This hope we have as an anchor of the soul, both sure and steadfast, and which enters the Presence behind the veil, where the forerunner has entered for us, even Jesus, having become High Priest forever according to the order of Melchizedek* (Hebrews 6:19-20).

This is the only place in the Bible where the word "forerunner" is mentioned, and it is attributed to Jesus and the new priesthood that He established for us to follow. Forerunner is the Greek word *prodromos*. The definition in Strong's Greek Dictionary paints a powerful picture:

> 4274 pródromos (from 4253 /pró, "before" and 1408 /drómos, "a race-course") – properly, a person running ahead (a forerunner) to reach the destination before others – i.e., arriving safely in advance for the benefit of others who also need to get there.

I love this. Jesus as our Forerunner ran ahead of us to reach the destination before us. He ran ahead to the heavenly tabernacle in advance for the benefit of us "who also need to get there." We need to reach this heavenly tabernacle where the Father in all of His glory dwells, and where He rules on His heavenly throne. Jesus, our Forerunner, paved the way.

In the Old Testament temple, the high priest was the only one allowed to enter the Holy of Holies, which was sectioned off by a thick, beautiful veil that hung from ceiling to floor. In the Holy of Holies was the Ark of the Covenant, where the glory of God dwelt. The high priest was only permitted to enter the Holy of Holies once a year, and he could not enter without something very important: *blood.*

Jesus, our High Priest, entered behind the veil just as the high priest did in the Old Testament priesthood. However, after Jesus died, He did not enter the physical temple—which interestingly enough was the temple that Zerubbabel had built—but the *heavenly* temple. And He did not enter that heavenly temple with the blood of animals, but with *His own* blood.

> *Not with the blood of goats and calves, but with His own blood He entered the Most Holy Place once for all, having obtained eternal redemption* (Hebrews 9:12).

As the Forerunner, Jesus made a way for heaven and earth to connect again and now we can boldly enter the Holiest of All, the throne room where the Father dwells (Hebrews 10:19-22). Jesus became the High Priest forever in the order of the Melchizedek. This is the priesthood of Jesus that He foreran and initiated as a new pattern and model for us to follow so we can access the Presence behind the veil. Let us give ourselves fully to this revelation of how to live.

Melchizedek

So who is Melchizedek? Let's go back to Abraham's encounter in Genesis where Melchizedek makes his first, brief appearance.

> *For this Melchizedek, king of Salem, priest of the Most High God, who met Abraham returning from the slaughter of the kings and blessed him, to whom also Abraham gave a tenth part of all, first being translated "king of righteousness," and then also king of Salem, meaning "king of peace," without father, without mother, without genealogy, having neither beginning of days nor end of life, but made like the Son of God, remains a priest continually.*

Now consider how great this man was, to whom even the patriarch Abraham gave a tenth of the spoils (Hebrews 7:1-4).

The writer of Hebrews tells us some interesting facts about Melchizedek based on one brief encounter that he had with Abraham and the only time he appears in the Bible. His entire story consisted of three verses in Genesis chapter 14.

In the story, Abraham had settled with his family and tribe in Hebron, outside the city of Sodom and Gomorrah. There were two groups of kings that fought one another. One group prevailed against the kings of Sodom and Gomorrah and took their possessions and people, including Abraham's nephew, Lot. Abraham heard the news and took more than 300 of his trained men who were born in his house to rescue Lot. They defeat the five kings and their armies, rescue Lot, and are en route to bring back the possessions and people to the king of Sodom. Meanwhile, the king of Sodom hears of the victory and is en route to meet Abraham. Before they cross paths, Melchizedek shows up on the scene in the Valley of Shaveh, bringing Abraham wine and bread and blessing him, saying:

Blessed be Abram of God Most High, Possessor of heaven and earth; and blessed be God Most High, who has delivered your enemies into your hand (Genesis 14:19-20).

Abraham is so overwhelmed by the goodness and kindness of this man that he spontaneously gives him a tenth of everything that he rescued. He sowed a seed and tapped into Kingdom resources. Afterward, the covenant with God transpired, Sarah became a mother, and Abraham served as a priest-intercessor between God and humankind to try to save Sodom and Gomorrah.

The writer of Hebrews tells us that Melchizedek is the king of Salem, which is the former name of Jerusalem, the capital of Israel. Salem means "peace," and Melchizedek means "king of righteousness," so he is called king of peace and righteousness.

He was without genealogy, without mother or father, without beginning of days or end of life but resembling the Son of God and continuing as a priest forever. We can discern from this information that Melchizedek is a preincarnate Christ, appearing to reveal the sacrifice of His blood and His body to the father of our faith. So Jesus in preincarnate form showed even the patriarchs the importance of how He functions in two roles of both priest and king. He serves Abraham through serving the bread and wine, which were symbolic of the body and blood of Himself. It is the same scene at the Last Supper where Jesus blesses His disciples at the Passover dinner, gave thanks and gave them the bread saying, *"This is My body which is given for you; do this in remembrance of Me,"* and then He took the cup after supper, saying, *"This cup is the new covenant in My blood, which is shed for you"* (Luke 22:19-20).

The body and blood were symbolic of the new covenantal priesthood. He shed His *blood* that gives us access to the Presence behind the veil, that we could ascend into the Holiest of All, the throne room of heaven. While we are in that place, we are given our daily *bread* to descend and feed the lost and starving earth. This is the heaven-to-earth prayer that Jesus told us to pray in Matthew 6. He told us to worship the Father to open the gates of heaven so we can go in by the blood, and then bring back the *truth* of His Spirit's words, the bread that comes down from heaven to rule and reign on the earth. It is written in the *new song* from heaven in Revelation 5. It is the great dance of intimacy and ruling. It is the priest and king reality that God told Moses that He desired for Israel in Exodus 19:5-6:

> *"Now therefore, if you will indeed obey My voice and keep My covenant, then you shall be a special treasure to Me above all people; for all the earth is Mine. And you shall be to Me a kingdom of priests and a holy nation." These are the words which you shall speak to the children of Israel.*

Melchizedek was both a king and a priest. *The order of Melchizedek, then, is functioning in both the role of a priest and the role of a king.* This is how Jesus our High Priest lived, and this is how we as His Kingdom of priests are called to live as well.

The New Temple and the New Priesthood

The writer of Hebrews in chapters 5-10, quotes Psalm 110 several times leading up to the main point of the whole book: *this priesthood of Melchizedek is the ultimate place of maturity and the fullness of our experience of Christ within humanity.*

> *The Lord has sworn and will not relent, "You are a priest forever according to the order of Melchizedek"* (Psalm 110:4).

Jesus is our High Priest in the order of Melchizedek, and we who are His Kingdom of priests are to function in the same order. Those functioning in the Melchizedek priesthood are Christ men and Christ women of faith, believing the truth of this internal life in Christ who have entered into a supernatural rest and authority. Hebrews chapters 11-13 point to the fathers of the faith as an example of those who in the Old Testament preemptively saw this new way and were able to live accordingly. Hebrews describes the following:

- The sacrifices of Jesus' life and death were in the order of the Melchizedek priesthood activities. He learned obedience through suffering, sacrificing Himself for our sins. In this, He was perfected, becoming the Author of Salvation to all who obey Him.

- We have been called by God to this order of priesthood since the beginning of time. This is who Adam was, a son—one who was near God with heavenly access and obedience in the earth until the fall. Jesus was the Forerunner who would restore us to this priesthood.

- We are admonished to progress from babes in the faith in order to have the revelation and understanding of this priesthood. We must press through the foundations of the faith to grasp and apprehend this deeper reality of *identity* of whom we are not just functioning in the gifts or repentance but identity as those who mirror this priesthood.

- Jesus said that God answers the prayers of the righteous. Hebrews tells us that functioning in the order of the Melchizedek priesthood, we will be rightly aligned with heaven and do the will of the Father, and our prayers will be answered.

- As Jesus foreran as King of righteousness and peace *and* as the High Priest, He made *us* kings of righteousness and peace and priests to God. Hebrews tells us that we now have access to the same level of intimacy that He has with our Father. We are seated with Christ and He is seated at the right hand of the Father. He is our High Priest who entered into the Holiest of All and made that place available to all whom He calls. This is the place of the Father's lap, where we can go to Him, carrying all our cares and prayers, laying our heads on His chest. It is also the place of the Father's throne, where we can access and release His power and authority on earth as it is in heaven.

Therefore, brethren, having boldness to enter the Holiest by the blood of Jesus, by a new and living way which He consecrated for us, through the veil, that is, His flesh, and having a High Priest over the house of God, let us draw near with a true heart in full assurance of faith, having our hearts sprinkled from an evil conscience and our bodies washed with pure water (Hebrews 10:19-22).

A House of Prayer for All Nations

God declared that His house would be *"a house of prayer for all nations"* (Isaiah 56:7). God's people would be a people of prayer, a holy priesthood that enters into the Holiest of All in heaven. However, in today's seeker-friendly, homogenous churches, we have kept our people in the state of immaturity and external religious practices, not allowing them to grow up to access this realm in God. They have a form of godliness but lack power. They function in the exterior works of the temple, having a prayer life based on emergency needs.

When Jesus fashioned a whip and turned over the tables in the temple in Jerusalem, He quotes Isaiah 56:7, *"Is it not written, 'My house shall be called a house of prayer for all nations?' But you have made it a 'den of thieves'"* (Mark 11:17). The Greek word for *den* means a hiding place. Jesus is saying that His human temple is created for the purpose of love and connection with the Father, leading us into the greatness for which we were created. But when we don't pray, the thief comes in to hide within us, stealing the promises and purposes that are planned.

Many sincere believers today in our churches have their prayer lists, but have not tapped into the beauty realm and carried it back to earth. Jesus died to give us a new and living way. Our ministry is similar to that of the angels: we ascend as priests and descend in our roles as kings. As Zechariah 4 in essence states to Zerubbabel, "This new and living way will not come by the might or strength of the human mind or even disciplines, but through the Spirit and resting in Him, enabling us to reign as kings in the earth."

To summarize David Baron's thought on Zechariah 4, the Holy Spirit must be the only resource in the task of rebuilding the temple, which shall be visible proof of restored fellowship between God and His people; and hence, preparation for the accomplishment of us being the light of the nations.[1] This is a very offensive way of living, not adopted by many because it eliminates their might and strength, hence their pride of life, their ownership, and their identities as success-driven achievers. We are called to be houses of prayer, not houses of performance.

> *Also the sons of the foreigner who join themselves to the LORD, to serve Him, And to love the name of the LORD, to be His servants—everyone who keeps from defiling the Sabbath [rest], and holds fast My covenant—even them I will bring to My holy mountain, and make them joyful in My house of prayer. Their burnt offerings and their sacrifices will be accepted on My altar; for My house shall be called a house of prayer for all nations (Isaiah 56:6-7).*

Statistics tell us that the majority of church leadership don't spend a lot of time in prayer. The burden of the ministry has stolen their first love. Therefore, if they are not tasting of the good place in God, how can they lead us there? If they do not have this revelation, how can they function in this kind of authority? These churches are based on the needs of the people not leading them into prayer where the Teacher, Counselor, and Helper will take care of the majority of their needs and all we will have to do is file around the edges.

When I began our house of prayer, the Lord said, "If you teach them to pray, you don't have to tell them how to live." Today, I admonish you, don't forsake the place of resting in God—prayer—and entering into the Holiest of All, spending time with the Creator of the universe, taking your cares to Him, letting Him tell you how much He delights in you and His pleasure of loving you. You will be changed into the perfect reflection of His Son as you gaze on Him, becoming the very image of God, His sons and daughters that all creation is waiting to see. Then and only then will you make His enemies His footstool and turn the kingdom of this world into the Kingdom of our God. Within a life of prayer, comes the free flowing anointing oil. This anointing is a fully functioning Christ, which means Anointed One, in us, the hope of glory. The oiliness is what breaks the yoke and makes all things possible that are impossible.

Tabernacle of David

The tabernacle of David gives us more insight to this king-priest ministry of the order of Melchizedek.

Amos prophesies that the fallen tabernacle of David will be rebuilt and its damages repaired, its ruins raised up so they can possess the remnant of Edom and all the Gentiles who are called by His name (Amos 9:11). James quotes this Scripture in Acts 15 as the apostles and elders start seeing a multitude of Gentiles come into the Kingdom. James knew that in some way this tabernacle of David was being rebuilt in his day; and as a result, Gentiles were coming to seek the Lord.

What I find interesting is that Amos says "the tabernacle of David" will be rebuilt, not the temple of Solomon. What is it about the nature of the tabernacle of David over the temple of Solomon that God would restore to draw the nations to Himself?

The temple of Solomon was built with the finest wood and ornate with gold, silver, and precious stones. The tabernacle of David, however, was a mere tent that David had raised up in the City of David. I believe it is the tent with its simplicity of closeness and intimacy that God wants to restore. David built the tent in his own backyard for the Ark of the Covenant.

The Ark of the Covenant was kept in the Holy of Holies. It was where the glory and presence of God dwelt among the people of Israel. It was constructed during the time of Moses, and it was significant for Israel's prosperity and victory in battle throughout the times of the judges of Israel. Because of the holiness and glory of God present in the Ark, God set up a particular order in which it was to be transported from one place to another.

King David wanted to recover the Ark to be near to the presence of the Lord to minister to the Lord. This tabernacle of David is symbolic of the tabernacle/temple described in Hebrews 9:11, the temple not made by hands that would operate in the Melchizedek priesthood. The Melchizedek priesthood is only mentioned twice in the Old Testament, yet the book of Hebrews focuses on this being the priesthood of Jesus.

King David is an example of someone who functioned as priest and king and the resulting prosperity, peace, dominion through his life in God. David operating in the order of Melchizedek is key to how to bring God's presence and all God's promises into our lives. Let's look at the author of Psalm 110.

David's greatest desire was to dwell in the house of the Lord all the days of his life, to be near the presence of the Lord. After he captured Jerusalem from the Philistines, he made it the capital and decided to make that his residence. The first thing he did after he was crowned king was to bring the presence of the Lord, the Ark of the Covenant, back to Jerusalem. So once again the king of Salem (peace) would reign. David was eager to welcome God's presence back into the midst of His people.

Saul had been king for a long time and prospered by the hand of God, yet he never had the desire to get the Ark of His presence from the Philistines who took it from Eli and his sons. He cared more about his position and political power than being near God.

But David's heart had a longing for the nearness of God and the people agreed:

> *"It is time to bring back the Ark of our God, for we neglected it during the reign of Saul." The whole assembly agreed to this, for the people could see it was the right thing to do. So David summoned all Israel, from the Shihor Brook of Egypt in the south all the way to the town of Lebo-hamath in the north, to join in bringing the Ark of God from Kiriath-jearim* (1 Chronicles 13:3-5 NLT).

David had a focused and purposed desire. His passion is described well in Psalm 42:1-3:

> *As the deer pants for the water brooks, so pants my soul for You, O God. My soul thirsts for God, for the living God. When shall I come and appear before God? My tears have been my food day and night, while they continually say to me, "Where is your God?"*

For David, the greatest reward of being made king was bringing the Ark of God's presence close to himself and his people. It is clear to see why David is considered to be God's favorite as his one desire was to be near to God, not riches or influence or nations, but the Presence!

Whereas the Lord was eager to dwell among His people, there was divine order prescribed for carrying the Ark. As the Ark journeyed in the oxen-led cart, there was great anticipation from David and the priests as they sang and danced with jubilee. However, the oxen stumbled and his beloved priest, Uzzah reached out his hand to steady the Ark and was struck dead instantly. David was devastated because the Lord's anger burst out at Uzzah. David instructed for the Ark to be placed in the house of Obed-edom of Gath.

> *David was now afraid of God, and he asked, "How can I ever bring the Ark of God back into my care?" So David did not move the Ark into the City of David. Instead, he took it to the house of Obed-edom of Gath. The Ark of God remained there in Obed-edom's house for three months, and the Lord*

blessed the household of Obed-edom and every-
thing he owned (1 Chronicles 13:12-14 NLT).

With great sorrow, David returned to Jerusalem, wres-
tling with how he would get near to God. If the priest cannot
even touch the Ark, how can he dwell with the presence of
the Lord? Like Jesus, David is not from the Levitical tribe but
from the Tribe of Judah. During the three months, David
must have taken to meditation; and as a prophetic psalm-
ist, I believe he witnessed an eternal conversation in heaven
between the Trinity, revealed in Psalm 110:

> *The Lord said to my Lord, "Sit at My right hand,*
> *till I make Your enemies Your footstool." The Lord*
> *shall send the rod of Your strength out of Zion. Rule*
> *in the midst of Your enemies! Your people shall be*
> *volunteers in the day of Your power; in the beau-*
> *ties of holiness, from the womb of the morning, You*
> *have the dew of Your youth. The Lord has sworn*
> *and will not relent, "You are a priest forever accord-*
> *ing to the order of Melchizedek." The Lord is at*
> *Your right hand; He shall execute kings in the day*
> *of His wrath. He shall judge among the nations, He*
> *shall fill the places with dead bodies, He shall exe-*
> *cute the heads of many countries. He shall drink of*
> *the brook by the wayside; therefore He shall lift up*
> *the head.*

Dr. Francis Myles, in his book *The Order of Melchizedek*,
connects this psalm to David's attempt to bring the Ark of the
Covenant into Jerusalem. He writes:

To David's complete surprise, the divine conversation within the Godhead was centered on a heavenly priesthood which was not functioning in its official capacity in the nation of Israel.... David realized that God also had a driving desire to be touched by His people and to live among them. David realized that he had discovered the most powerful priestly Order that operates from within the realms of eternity. David could clearly see that under this priestly Order of Melchizedek, Christ was the everlasting High Priest and that there was no veil of restriction between God and His people. David also realized that under this priestly Order every one of God's holy children can hear the voice of God and walk in His divine power in the beauty of holiness.[2]

David's Successful Procession

After his first failed attempt to bring the Ark of God's presence into Jerusalem, David received revelation that God's presence, or anointing, will only come through this order of Melchizedek. So David prepared a place for the Ark and built a tent in his backyard. He brought in the Ark in the order commanded by God; the priests were sanctified, and they shed the blood of bulls and rams along the journey before the Ark.

David put on the same fine linen robe as the priests and wore the linen ephod. The linen ephod was a type of apron worn on the breastplate of the High Priest, with stones that represent the twelve tribes and the Urim and Thummim.

As the King, David took on the role of the High Priest as he danced and escorted the Ark of God's presence into his back-yard. I believe he touched the eternal plan of God in Psalm 110, and in doing so accessed the new and living way described by the writer of Hebrews.

David became the most successful king in all of history. Through this new and living way, his people lived in peace from their enemies on all sides, were the richest nation on the earth, dwelled in the midst of the presence of God, and had a just king ruling over them. Just as David had divine inspiration of how to bring the Ark of God's presence into his life and the lives of his people, so we today can learn from this revelation. As we function in the order of Melchizedek as both king and priest, we can be assured of the same outcome and success.

Error of Worldwide Theocracies

In the heart of all humankind is the hidden truth of who we are created to be and how we are created to live. You can see this truth through the ages as humans have attempted to replicate the priest and king model of governmental authority. Starting with Constantine, efforts were made to create a church and state reality that would govern the people through the Roman Catholic Church working with the king. Down through time, this has been modeled with other theocracies: Hinduism in India; Buddha in Asia; Islam throughout the Middle East with Sharia law; even in the United States through its Judeo-Christian values influencing our laws and democracy.

We understand that the only way to rule and reign is to work through a priest and king mandate. Theocracies and church-state relationships throughout history have most often perverted this king-priest reality that God has embedded deep within humanity. The state and Church have used each other to satisfy a lust for power and control or to bring about heaven on earth—not by the Spirit, but by human might and power—political and military strength. But God is teaching this generation what the true expression of this king-priest reality is to look like.

Endnotes

1. David Baron, *Zechariah: A Commentary on His Visions and Prophecies*, (Grand Rapids, MI: Kregel Publications), 137.
2. Francis Myles, *The Order of Melchizedek: Rediscovering the Eternal Royal Priesthood of Jesus Christ* (Arlington, TX: Ancient Times Publishers), 46.

9

LIVING AS KINGS AND PRIESTS: GOD'S CHOSEN GOVERNMENT

I want to reiterate a couple of important sentences from the last chapter. *The order of Melchizedek is the functioning of God's people in both the role of a king and the role of a priest.* This is how Jesus our High Priest lived, and this is how we as His Kingdom of priests are called to live, as well. I believe the lack of living in and through this lifestyle is the reason so many Christians live below their potential and have unfulfilled prophecies in their lives which has led to disappointment and even sometimes falling away from the faith. They are waiting on God to break-through and He is waiting for them to seek first His Kingdom and learn how to live in righteousness—His ways—partnering with Him to bring their breakthrough into the earth.

In the vision that the Lord gave to Zerubbabel in Zechariah 4, the trees had two branches that poured the anointing into the candlestick, the seven churches. So the branches/trees represent the two branches that make up the governmen-tal authority of heaven on the earth. As I mentioned before, there are three branches in the U.S. government: executive, legislative, and judicial. Each of the branches of government have duties that pertain to their respective branches, and they are designed to flow together as one to accomplish the goal of governing.

Likewise, the two branches of the government of heaven, the priestly and kingly branches, involve certain functions meant to operate together. Most of the Church sees these two roles as two occupations. They believe the role of the priests are for those who serve in the church and the role of the kings are those who serve in the marketplace. This is 100 percent wrong. The new priesthood is every believer; an internal governance that influences external reality. This internal government replaced the law that ruled God's people through behavioral management. The law has now gone inward and is written on our hearts.

> *For this is the covenant that I will make with the house of Israel after those days, says the Lord; I will put My laws in their mind and write them on their hearts; and I will be their God and they shall be My people* (Hebrews 8:10).

The main functions of priests and kings can be understood as the following:

Priests: Worship, Prayer, Thanksgiving

The function of the priestly branch of God's government is to fill up the bowls in heaven through *worship, prayer, and giving thanks* to God for who He is, what He is doing and has done. The priests offer up thanksgiving and praise and enter into His presence and use their eyes and ears to *see* and *hear* what is in heaven.

Kings: Prophecy, Intercession, Preaching the Gospel through Power

The function of the kingly branch of God's government is to use their mouths to release *prophecy, intercession, and preaching the gospel of the kingdom* with power and healing. As kings, they *speak* and *release* what they see and hear in their roles as priests. Their priestly prayers are poured out through the kingly declarations of their mouths. They will steward what God is doing in heaven with works of faith.

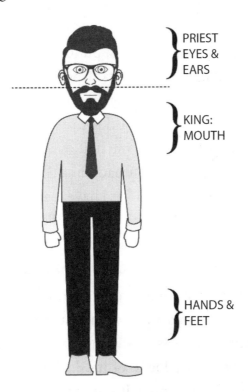

PRIEST EYES & EARS

KING: MOUTH

HANDS & FEET

We are not supposed to be either priests *or* kings—we are both working together. One expression without the other will not be the governmental authority that God designed through the life and sacrifice of Jesus, and we will not reign on earth with Christ. I give you some practical applications and testimonies later.

The plan of God to fill the earth with His glory is you and me in Christ. Christ, the Anointed One, living inside us functioning in the order of the Melchizedek priesthood, and creating us to be one with Him in this spiritual dance. Jesus came and initiated the new man, the new priesthood, and a new way of life to function as new creations filled with the glory of God inside.

The Melchizedek Order of priests and kings means we are agents of the impossible in the earth doing the will of our Father. We are like the Avengers, but our power comes from within. One of the most important points of this life is the statement Jesus made in Matthew 11:30, *"My yoke is easy and My burden is light."* However, I don't see that in the Church. I see three things: 1) religious activities with no power, 2) a power movement with no intimacy, and 3) prayer movement with few answered prayers. What I have seen is that the priests don't like the kings and the kings don't like the priests. They have separated themselves as if they are supposed to be separate. The Lord said that He made us to be both.

I was recently in a small group setting with leaders from two ministries. One was a prayer ministry and the other was a missions ministry. I was sitting in between them and heard the most interesting dialogue of masked accusations toward the way each was functioning. It was really heartbreaking. The ones who see themselves only, or primarily, as priests believe that spending their time in prayer is the most important role, and those who see themselves only as kings believe spreading the gospel or ruling is the most important. As Reinhard Bonnke, who has one of the most successful ministries of all time, says, "A one legged man cannot run very far." Both roles are necessary to advance God's Kingdom.

Marketplace People as Both Kings and Priests

I have seen this same misconception occur with marketplace Christians. The people in the marketplace believe that the priests are the leaders in the Church while they themselves are the kings in the marketplace. I have also heard it said that they, as marketplace people, are priests on Sunday and kings on Monday through Friday. This is a grave error. Again, it relies on external function instead of internal role. It is again isolating the role of the priests in a prayerful experience limited to one day a week. They don't have the revelation that every believer is *both* a priest and king *every day*. It would be like saying you are only going to be a parent when you are at home, yet when you go to work, you are not a parent. You function in the role of a parent because you have children, not because of your location or occupation.

Jesus came to take authority of the high places, the seven mountains of influence. The Church, the *ecclesia* (the sent-out ones), is a transformative people who are sent out into the world to create change through influence. The seven mountains are the church, business, family, government, arts and entertainment, education, and media. Christians who are doctors, teachers, stay-at-home parents, plumbers, politicians, students, and reporters, etc. are *all* created to function as *priests and kings*. There will be no dominion until we make these spheres of influence and kingdoms of this earth, the Kingdoms of our God.

I have heard from many in the marketplace, especially men, several reasons why they cannot function as priests. First, they think they don't hear and see the way many "prophets" hear and see, so therefore they are not qualified to function in their priesthood. Second, they don't have time to pray. Third, they are engrossed in the worldly system of business and do not understand how a life of prayer can benefit them.

First, *if you feel like you don't see or hear often or clearly:* I want to challenge you to know that if you are a born-again believer and baptized in the Holy Spirit, you have the ability to see and hear. Paul says in Ephesians 2:18, *"For through Him* [Christ] *we both have access by one Spirit to the Father."* All Christians have access to the Father. If you want to hear and see, *you have to pray.* You cannot turn a light on unless you connect it to a power source. Ask the Holy Spirit how many hours a week you are to pray, then be obedient to what you think you hear. Trust in what you hear and obey. Sometimes I hear a small voice, sometimes it's booming. I follow both. As my pastor, Terry Moore from Sojourn Church, says, "God is more able to lead you than you are to follow Him."

Second, *if you feel as if you don't have time to pray:* I was challenged by the Lord to begin my life in prayer at one of the most desperate times of my life when I had no time, energy, or money. Our daughter, Bliss, had an accident and broke her neck. She was a quadriplegic. We had just brought her home from the hospital and I was her full-time caregiver. I had six other children and was in part-time ministry, and John had his own budding business. The Lord kept saying to me, "Build My house of prayer." I repeatedly told Him that I was kind of busy, but He persisted.

I asked the Lord to teach me to pray, and He said to begin to pray twelve hours a week, three hours at a time. So I heard this and thought, *What? I don't have twelve minutes in a day.* I wasn't totally sure if this was God, but I was sure the devil was not telling me to pray for twelve hours a week. Then there was the other option, *What if it's just my imagination?* I can assure you, if you think it's just you, go with it anyway, because even if by chance it is, God will honor your desire to be obedient. My journey was hard for the first few times of three-hour prayer times but they turned into the richest, most enjoyable experience of my life. The benefit was my life began to turn around, and all the weightiness, difficulties, and impossibilities of my life circumstances began to change, and supernaturally I had free and available time every day. I was energized and had hope again.

I believe this issue of *time* is the most challenging of all three obstacles to the lifestyle of king-priest. You have to take a leap of faith to intentionally decrease your availability to the world to increase the presence of God in your life, hence, favor and anointing. The Lord gave me a dream where John and I were giving away 20 percent of our house to a newly married couple. I was speaking to the contractor and asking him if our master bedroom was going to be decreased in size, he gave the most amazing and biblical answer. He said, "No I have used a special formula in calculating the size of your master bedroom. It contains an algorithm that when you divide, it actually creates multiplication and now your master bedroom will be even bigger than it was in the beginning." The concept of giving God your time will net you great reward and you will be increased. It's like pulling back the bow to shoot you out as an arrow.

In addition to people who think they can't hear from God or don't have time to pray, I think there is another group of people within marketplace Christians. Third, *these are people who have a head knowledge of this truth but lack a heart revelation.* They know that prayer is important for Christians, but they lack a daily and consistent prayer life. They are focused on their call or mission to the marketplace and don't understand how to fit this necessary lifestyle of priest-king into their busy lives or if it will even truly benefit them in the workplace.

They may believe in a supernatural God who heals or who prophesies, but they struggle to apply the supernatural to their own sphere of marketplace influence. They do not have the revelation of God as the great Creator in the marketplace and ready to mentor them so they can be successful.

They have difficulty grasping the productivity of prayer and releasing the words of God over their lives—how God builds not by might nor power but *through the Spirit.*

Remember David. He was called to the mountain of government as king of Israel. He had daily duties of administration, governing, going to war, securing the borders, etc. But David, a man after God's own heart, set his heart on one main thing: to spend time in the presence of the Lord and to seek His counsel. David pours out his heart to the Lord in Psalm 27:4 saying,

One thing I have desired of the Lord, that will I seek: that I may dwell in the house of the Lord all the days of my life, to behold the beauty of the Lord, and to inquire in His temple.

The wisdom David received to release the greatest amount of heavenly influence in the mountain of government as *king* flowed from his desire and commitment to give himself to this life as a *priest* who ministered to the Lord in prayer. Read about David's life in First and Second Samuel, about how he met with the Lord and asked for specific wisdom for specific situations. Marketplace men and women, we need you out there as *kings* in your mountain of influence where God has sent you. But you will be much more effective and prosperous in bringing the Kingdom of heaven into your sphere if you take the time as a *priest* to meet with the King of kings. Your sphere of influence matters to the Lord, and He wants to speak to you about it. He wants to give you the story He wrote for you so you can read it into the earth. Daily, He gives you words about your life and then you repeat them throughout your day until they are fulfilled.

What if God spoke to you about business plans, partnerships, financial management, and opportunities for increase? What if instead of anxiously trying to figure out how to solve problems, the Lord would speak to you about what to do? What if the Holy Spirit showed you how to spend your time most effectively for the greatest amount of return? This can only happen when we take the time to meet with the Lord. Where we enjoy His presence and seek His counsel.

This is how David was successful, this is how Jesus was successful, and this is how you will be successful. This is the order of Melchizedek. This is building according to the Spirit. I give more detailed instruction about how to implement this practically later in the book. The apostle Paul talks about this new way of living in Colossians 3:10 (NIV), *"and have put on the new self, which is renewed in knowledge in the image of its Creator."*

Paul addressed the offensive nature of the "not by might, nor by power but by My Spirit" lifestyle—this new way of the Spirit and of the new self in Kingdom living—in Ephesians 4:17-19:

> *This I say, therefore, and testify in the Lord, that you should no longer walk as the rest of the Gentiles walk, in the futility of their mind, having their understanding darkened, being alienated from the life of God, because of the ignorance that is in them, because of the blindness of their heart; who, being past feeling, have given themselves over to lewdness* [carnality or excess], *to work* [labor or job] *all uncleanness* [impure motives] *with greediness.*

The world seeks monetary gain through its own carnal understanding with impure motives of selfish ambition and greediness. Paul describes the condition and then gives the prescription for the new priesthood: renewal in the mind as Joshua was in Zechariah chapter 3, where his dirty garments were removed and he was given a clean turban for his head, representing a renewed mind and garments of righteousness.

That, however, is not the way of life you learned when you heard about Christ and were taught in him in accordance with the truth that is in Jesus. You were taught, with regard to your former way of life, to put off your old self, which is being corrupted by its deceitful desires; to be made new in the attitude of your minds; and to put on the new self, created to be like God in true righteousness and holiness (Ephesians 4:20-24 NIV).

Paul is describing the new self who is not subject to the system of the earth but is aligned with the Holy Spirit; therefore, the anointing is large in them creating opportunity and favor. If you are asking for breakthrough, it resides inside you, because He lives in you. Favor is not fairy dust; it is the anointing that breaks the yoke or resistance to prosperity and opens doors. Remember, Christ means *anointed One*. There is a direct correlation between prayer and the measure of His presence within you. Small Christ inside, small life outside. Big Christ inside, big life outside. In other words, turn off the TV and turn on your gaze toward Jesus.

As it was with David and Jesus, so it will be with you as you operate in the Melchizedek priesthood model. The Ark of God's presence will be with you, you will prosper financially and relationally, and you will have entered into His rest. It may sound like foolishness, but embracing this lifestyle as a king-priest will fill you with the wisdom and power of God. The children of God are led by the Spirit of God. God is training us in these last days to function as king-priests, and the glory of God is about to be seen on us like never before.

Kings and Priests in the Capstone Generation

A major sign that we are in the capstone generation—the generation before the Lord returns—is the emergence of these kings and priests who will overcome the enemy and reign with Christ on the earth forever. I believe the battle at the end of the age will be between satan's army of kings and priests and *Christ's* army of kings and priests. Once the saints begin to function in their governmental roles in the order of Melchizedek, the glory of God will be poured out greater than at any other time in all of history.

God needs His governmental temples in operation so they can contain this level of power and authority. The Church is faltering, not because of a lack of activity but because of a lack of revelation. If God is releasing revelation about the rebuilding of Zerubbabel's temple and His priesthood of Melchizedek, we know that we are the generation of His return.

Right before Jesus went to the cross, the disciples asked Him, "What will be the sign of Your coming and of the end of the age?" He tells them that there will be signs and shakings in the earth (natural disasters, famines, wars, economic crises, outbreaks of diseases), the blossoming of the fig tree (which I believe to be Israel), the persecution of believers, and His faithful servants preaching the gospel to the ends of the earth (Matthew 24:3-35). His last-days messengers will be communicating to His Church the need to *watch* in the season of Israel's reemergence and in the generation of His triumphant return (Matthew 24:36-50).

Jesus says in Matthew, *"Watch therefore, for you do not know what hour your Lord is coming"* (Matthew 24:42). Jesus then shares two parables describing the roles of His priests and kings who will be on earth before He returns. He shares in Matthew 25:1-13 about the importance of having a life of anointing (oil) through intimacy and prayer *as priests* in the parable of the wise and foolish virgins. The priesthood on the earth on the day of His return will know how to access heaven. They will see and hear what the Father is saying and doing.

Next, He shares in Matthew 25:14-30 about the importance of stewarding "talents" as kings and understanding how to distribute, invest, and sow the seeds from our time in prayer as priests. We must be faithful to listen and see and understand how to transform the earth with His seeds of money, gifts, and words. Those who are faithful with little will "rule over many things" (Matthew 25:23) *as kings*. They will function in the mysteries of the wisdom of the Kingdom ways of sowing and reaping. They will understand how to multiply seeds and bring forth a harvest. They will bring heaven's resources to earth to see transformation.

The seed is described in Scripture as both money and words. While the parable of the talents (money) does not specifically mention the talents as words, I believe it can also apply. As we faithfully steward the words that the Lord has given us and build with those words, He can trust us to rule and reign with Him as kings.

Before Jesus comes back to the earth, He is calling and commissioning the last generation to live in this order of Melchizedek that He modeled for us: to live as priests and kings. I believe we are the generation that will operate in these roles. As we learn to operate in this lifestyle of kings and priests, we will be empowered to confront the darkness coming in the last days and usher in the return of Christ.

10

BEWARE OF BABYLON

The House of Zerubbabel was built in Jerusalem, a stronghold of Babylon.

Remember in the beginning of my encounters with the Holy Spirit, Babylon was emphasized. God said, "It's about Babylon," and showed me a pentagram, the satanic star. Babylon means confusion and comes from the root word, *balal,* meaning to mingle or have mixture. We have already talked about following God and His ways and being free from this confusion.

In this chapter, I give a stern warning to this generation: BEWARE OF BABYLON. Babylon is the earthly culture, a system of knowledge created by satan to rule the earth. It is presented as wisdom and knowledge, but is not from heaven. It is from the earth for the earth and does not reproduce eternal fruit or righteousness. It deals in facts, not truth. There is a truth from heaven that rules and has power over earthly wisdom. This is God's plumb line.

God's heavenly system is the reproduction of God's will, ways, and words. It is the reproduction of heaven's truth and knowledge on the earth that has power over dark knowledge, even knowledge that presents itself as good. There are two armies on the earth right now. The Babylonian system is creating a demonic army of tares—and heaven is creating a heavenly army of wheat. This is the showdown at the end of the age. Joel speaks of these two armies that will be present at the end of the age in Joel 2.

The End-Time Babylonian Army

Blow the trumpet in Zion,
And sound an alarm in My holy mountain!
Let all the inhabitants of the land tremble;
For the day of the Lord is coming,
For it is at hand:
A day of darkness and gloominess,
A day of clouds and thick darkness,
Like the morning clouds spread over the mountains.
A people come, great and strong,
The like of whom has never been;
Nor will there ever be any such after them,
Even for many successive generations.
A fire devours before them,
And behind them a flame burns;
The land is like the Garden of Eden before them,
And behind them a desolate wilderness;
Surely nothing shall escape them.
Their appearance is like the appearance of horses;
And like swift steeds, so they run.
With a noise like chariots
Over mountaintops they leap,

*Like the noise of a flaming fire that devours the
stubble,
Like a strong people set in battle array.
Before them the people writhe in pain;
All faces are drained of color*
(Joel 2:1-6).

Joel prophesied about a Babylonian army coming against
Israel, the people of God. This army was powerful, organized,
and relentless in their destruction. He trumpeted a warning
to God's people to wake up and prepare for the coming of this
great and terrible army. But Joel's prophecy will be ultimately
fulfilled in the last days, before the day of the Lord's return to
the earth. This end-time Babylonian army will be led by the
most demonized man in human history—the antichrist—who
will ruthlessly war against God's people and bring destruction to the earth.

*And I saw the beast, the kings of the earth, and
their armies, gathered together to make war against
Him who sat on the horse and against His army*
(Revelation 19:19).

God is sounding the trumpet again today through His
prophets to alert the Body of Christ that a great and terrible
army is arising in the earth. This army operates out of the
Babylonian system of confusion. The ways of this Babylonian
system are so wickedly crafted that even Eve was deceived by
it in the Garden. She was not tempted by fruit but by the desire
for the knowledge of good and evil and to be "like God," even
though she was already made in His image and likeness. The

Babylonian system operates out of the knowledge of good and evil. This knowledge appeals to us because it causes us to feel empowered and in charge like God and desiring self-glorification. It elevates the human mind and human ways of thinking over the Spirit. It pridefully seeks to exalt itself against the knowledge of God and His ways (2 Corinthians 10:5).

So, let's look closer at how these two armies that Joel prophesies about are fueled by the increase of knowledge in the last days. Scripture tells us in the book of Daniel that in the last days, knowledge will increase.

> *But you Daniel, shut up the words, and seal the book until the time of the end; many shall run to and fro, and knowledge shall increase* (Daniel 12:4).

We can look around us and see that knowledge is increasing. We live in the information age and technology is increasing at exponential rates. Those feeding off the Babylonian system of dark knowledge of good and evil are becoming emboldened and many are gaining incredible wealth. There are some who have acquired more wealth than many nations and have submitted themselves to the beast, the antichrist, spoken of in Revelation 17. They are kings but have not received a kingdom. They know each other and are networking with plans of global domination based on their own designs on how the earth and God's people should be ruled.

> *The ten horns which you saw are ten kings who have received no kingdom as yet, but they receive authority for one hour as kings with the beast. These are of one mind, and they will give their power and*

authority to the beast. These will make war with the Lamb, and the Lamb will overcome them, for He is Lord of lords and King of kings; and those who are with Him are called, chosen, and faithful (Revelation 17:12-14).

These "kings" are not currently political heads of state, but they are behind the scenes controlling nations through their money and dark ideology of population control, international banking, earth's production, pharmaceuticals, and the development of a one-world government. The Bible says they receive authority for one hour of agreement and will try to overcome the Lord and His army. In their time of "authority," they raise up their Babylonian army to make war with God's end-time army, as we saw in Joel 2:1-10 and Revelation 19:19.

This Babylonian army is fierce, "a people great and strong." They strike terror in the hearts of the saints and those on the earth. They operate as counterfeit kings and priests, worshipping the beast and releasing his plans and lies into the earth to control this army and advance satan's end-time plans. Many worship satan and access his power through satanic rituals, including sacrifices with the blood of innocents and abominations of murder, sexual perversion, pedophilia, and cannibalism. Even when confronted with the power and judgments of God, they will not repent of their wickedness.

But the rest of mankind, who were not killed by these plagues, did not repent of the works of their hands, that they should not worship demons, and idols of gold, silver, brass, stone, and wood, which can neither see nor hear nor walk. And they did not repent of their murders or their sorceries or their sexual immorality or their thefts (Revelation 9:20-21).

We can see shaking and captivity happening today with so much confusion released from this demonic rulership. They use a war of words to create chaos and lawlessness. Words are shooting like arrows from politicians, the media, social media platforms, and even the many in the Church. They create confusion, fear, bondage, and lawlessness to fuel the violence of this army unto control. This army believes in the ways of self and earthly knowledge devoid of the wisdom of God.

The plans of Babylon sound like wisdom but believing and following these plans will lead to destruction, even for some of God's elect. Their objective is to rage against and destroy the Lord and His chosen and faithful. While they have come under the influence of the beast and are given authority for a limited time, they are actually fulfilling God's purpose (Revelation 17:17) by stirring up, waking up His sleeping bridal army. This Babylonian army rises up and begins to destroy and consume the inhabitants of the earth, but then the Lord steps in and His voice is heard by His remnant.

> *The Lord gives voice before His army; for His camp is very great; for strong is the One who executes His word. For the day of the Lord is great and very terrible; who can endure it?* (Joel 2:11)

The Holy Spirit is warning God's people to come away from this system of Babylon, or they will be overtaken by it. When Jesus came and tore the veil from heaven to earth through His death and resurrection, we can be led by the voice of the Holy Spirit. It is the breaking in of the voice of the Lord that calls to His army and awakens her to His plumb line and truth.

God's End-Time Army

"Now, therefore," says the LORD, "Turn to Me with all your heart, with fasting, with weeping, and with mourning" (Joel 2:12).

The voice of God, which is the plumb line of truth, is being restored to God's people, bringing clarity and hope. The first thing the voice of the Lord did in the book of Joel was to call God's people home to Himself at the heart level. Today, the Lord is redefining His Church as a temple built by His own hands where His Spirit dwells, not a building you attend on Sundays. God said to Israel in Joel's day, "Return to Me with all your heart." Church, God is again trumpeting His voice to us today saying, "Return to Me with all your heart." He wants *all* of our hearts.

In His words, "Return to Me with all your heart," He is saying to leave Babylon, the culture of this age, and come home to His trustworthy leadership. He is saying there can be no mixture in His Kingdom ways. He requires full allegiance. The days of being "of" the world are over. He is saying to His Church, "No mixture anymore." Your ways have to be "Not by might nor by power but by My Spirit." We have to *turn and bow* in humility and meekness. We live in the world but we cannot be of the world. We cannot continue to give our affection to and trust in the things of the world. We cannot continue to elevate our minds and our conclusions over the leadership of His Spirit.

> *So rend your heart, and not your garments; return to the LORD your God, for He is gracious and merciful, slow to anger, and of great kindness; and He relents from doing harm* (Joel 2:13).

God's Fivefold Promise

The promise to the Lord's army, for those who turn to the Lord wholeheartedly in this hour is fivefold. There will be the double portion of *grace* to pour out the following:

1. Grain, New Wine, and Oil

> *The Lord will answer and say to His people, "Behold, I will send you grain and new wine and oil, and you will be satisfied by them; I will no longer make you a reproach among the nations"* (Joel 2:19).

This represents the Promised Land provision given to the children of Israel for their obedience. Israel offered grain and new wine in the temple as a way of fellowshipping, of communing with the Lord. Jesus offered grain and new wine at the Last Supper, signifying His body and blood, as a way of communing with His disciples (1 Corinthians 10:16). The grain and new wine, then, is a promise of communion, union with God that strengthens and protects us as we follow Him even when faced with difficulty. The oil, as discussed in a previous chapter, is the anointing that produces power on our words and actions. The anointing is a yoke breaker, casting out demons, breaking off sickness and wrong thinking (Isaiah 10:27; Luke 4:18-19). It clears the path for healing, salvation, boldness, empowered teaching, and exponential increase.

The promise of grain, wine, and oil also appears in Deuteronomy and Haggai. The Jews historically kept a Mezuzah on the arch of the doorway which quotes Deuteronomy 11:13-14:

> *And it shall be that if you earnestly obey My commandments which I command you today, to love the LORD your God and serve Him with all your heart and with all your soul, then I will give you the rain for your land in its season, the early rain and the latter rain, that you may gather in your grain, your new wine, and your oil.*
>
> *Is the seed* [grain] *still in the barn? As yet the vine* [wine], *the fig tree, the pomegranate, and the olive tree* [oil] *have not yielded fruit. But from this day I will bless you* (Haggai 2:19).

This creates an internal strengthening of our spirits and strong connection with the Godhead. God desires a people who have turned to Him in love. His promise is to use us to destroy the enemy through our obedience and authority. He will tear down the Babylonian army as He makes His priests and kings rulers over His Kingdom.

> *Speak to Zerubbabel, governor of Judah, saying: "I will shake heaven and earth. I will overthrow the throne of kingdoms; I will destroy the strength of the Gentile kingdoms. I will overthrow the chariots*

and those who ride in them; the horses and their riders shall come down, every one by the sword of his brother. In that day," says the LORD of hosts, "I will take you, Zerubbabel My servant, the son of Shealtiel," says the LORD, "and will make you like a signet ring; for I have chosen you," says the LORD of hosts (Haggai 2:21-23).

2. Former and Latter Rain

Be glad then, you children of Zion, and rejoice in the Lord your God; for He has given you the former rain faithfully, and He will cause the rain to come down for you—the former rain, and the latter rain in the first month. The threshing floors shall be full of wheat, and the vats shall overflow with new wine and oil (Joel 2:23-24).

In this promise, God is not talking about water coming from the sky, He is speaking of knowledge and wisdom coming from heaven that will increase. This is the knowledge of God. The Word of God was made flesh and came down from heaven so that we could know the nature and character of God. In the flesh, we could relate to Him. He wasn't a distant image or unrelatable God. We could *know God.* He sent His only begotten Son to save us. God is supernatural. His words supersede *matter.* Even the waves obey Him. The more you know Him, the more you become like Him. The Bible tells us in Daniel:

> *But you, Daniel, shut up the words, and seal the book until the time of the end; many shall run to and fro, and knowledge shall increase* (Daniel 12:4).

I believe this former and latter rain speak of an outpouring of the knowledge of God. The army of God will have greater anointing and relational connection with God because knowledge is raining down in double measure. As we encounter the knowledge of who He is—His love, His mercy, His kindness, His nature, His power—more than any other generation; we will bow at the beauty of this experience. How is it even possible to be this close to and with Him. This is not knowledge that puffs up but knowledge that destroys pride. This is knowledge that destroys every lie and establishes the truth of who He is in His love and authority. We will be transformed into His likeness. This knowledge will explode in us like a nuclear bomb; and through this reality, we will do great exploits, not loving our lives unto death.

> *...but the people who know their God shall be strong, and carry out great exploits* (Daniel 11:32).

We will not play religious or political games because we are so plumbed in truth. As we roll into the last days, persecution and control will become more and more intense. How do we prosper during those times? *Increasing in the knowledge of God increases God in us and our understanding of how to speak to these things.* We will get wisdom on how to prosper in our souls, how to grow our businesses in times of hardship; we will thank Jesus for our food and watch it multiply. We will say, "STOP, GROW, MULTIPLY, LIVE, GO AWAY" and it will happen.

3. Restoring Provision

> The LORD says, "I will give you back what you lost to the swarming locusts, the hopping locusts, the stripping locusts, and the cutting locusts. It was I who sent this great destroying army against you. Once again you will have all the food you want, and you will praise the LORD your God, who does these miracles for you. Never again will my people be disgraced" (Joel 2:25-26 NLT).

God promises to strengthen His army by restoring to them all the resources that had been stolen during their times of rebellion. As we fully return our hearts without mixture back to God, He says He will bless our provision. He makes the same promise in Haggai to Zerubbabel, that while shaking has begun, in the midst of shaking He will pour out His provision, the silver and gold.

> I will shake all the nations, and the treasures of all the nations will be brought to this Temple. I will fill this place with glory, says the LORD of Heaven's Armies. The silver is mine, and the gold is mine, says the LORD of Heaven's Armies (Haggai 2:7-8 NLT).

4. The Spirit of Prophecy: Plumb Line of Truth

> And it shall come to pass afterward that I will pour out My Spirit on all flesh; your sons and your

daughters shall prophesy, your old men shall dream dreams, your young men shall see visions (Joel 2:28).

The voice of God, which is the plumb line of truth, is being restored to God's people, breaking in like a trumpet with clarity and hope. Just as it was when Haggai and Zechariah began to prophesy to God's people to rebuild Zerubbabel's temple, so it is now that God is declaring through His prophets that His finishing work of the capstone generation is at hand.

The promise of the outpouring of God's Spirit, not in the form of a short-lived revival but in the form of a transformative *awakening* will enable an explosion of the prophetic. Wisdom and knowledge will flow from heaven to earth like never before, and there will be great signs and wonders at the hand of God's governmental army. It will cause many to come into their right minds and millions will come into God's Kingdom filled with the zeal of the Lord. God will awaken His army so they are fully equipped to bring in His end-time harvest.

5. *The Glory of God*

"The glory of this latter temple shall be greater than the former," says the LORD of hosts. "And in this place I will give peace," says the LORD of hosts (Haggai 2:9).

As I mentioned in Chapter 7, the greater glory of God is reserved for the last generation. The promise of Zerubbabel's temple that was never poured out in the physical temple became a symbol of the glory of God being poured out at Pentecost, the former glory. The latter temple of our generation will be greater than that of the former foundational church. It is the increase of the knowledge of the love of God that transforms us from glory to glory.

> *That the God of our Lord Jesus Christ, the Father of glory, may give to you the spirit of wisdom and revelation in the knowledge of Him, the eyes of your understanding being enlightened; that you may know what is the hope of His calling, what are the riches of the glory of His inheritance in the saints* (Ephesians 1:17-18).

Scripture connects the intimate relationship between the Father and the Son and their desire for us to come into this Triune relationship. As the knowledge of God increases in our generation, we will be caught up into this great love. This love will cast out all fear and we will surrender to love, creating a fearless army of love-sick warriors. The glory will shine out of us that we surrendered all to the One we fully believe and trust. Jesus speaks to God about us:

> *And the glory which You gave Me I have given them, that they may be one just as We are one: I in them, and You in Me; that they may be made perfect in one, and that the world may know that You have sent Me, and have loved them as You have loved Me. Father, I desire that they also whom You gave Me may be with Me where I am, that they may behold My glory which You have given Me; for You loved Me before the foundation of the world* (John 17:22-24).

Two Olive Branches Shining in the Last Days

Satan is establishing an order of Babylonian kings and priests to release hell on earth. The only way for the Church to stand firm against them is by starting to mature now as God's kings and priests, serving in the power and authority of our High Priest and King Jesus Christ to release heaven on earth. Only heaven's authoritative words wielded by His chosen and faith-filled army will withstand the coming deluge of demonic onslaught.

The Lord is redefining His Church in our day as a living temple built by His own hands where His Spirit dwells, not a man-made building you attend on Sundays. Both Joshua and Zerubbabel, who were God's chosen king and priest, had to come out of Babylon and rebuild the temple in the midst of opposition from the Babylonian system. Joshua, in his role as priest, was cleansed so His mind wasn't connected to the culture but connected to the Kingdom. Zerubbabel was granted the double portion of grace to withstand opposition and complete the building of the temple.

Today, God is cleansing His people as priests and empowering them as kings to complete the building of God's end-time temple that He established at Pentecost. Even though we are surrounded on every side with darkness that shall cover the earth, it is the greatest hour for the Lamb and His saints to overcome. Like the shining lampstands in Zechariah's vision, God's priests and kings will shine with light and the glory of God.

Arise, shine; for your light has come! And the glory of the LORD is risen upon you. For behold, the darkness shall cover the earth, and deep darkness the people; but the LORD will arise over you, and His glory will be seen upon you (Isaiah 60:1-2).

11

THE PLUMB LINE IN THE HANDS OF ZERUBBABEL

Thus He showed me: Behold, the Lord stood on a wall made with a plumb line, with a plumb line in His hand. And the LORD said to me, "Amos, what do you see?" And I said, "A plumb line." Then the Lord said: "Behold, I am setting a plumb line in the midst of My people Israel; I will not pass by them anymore."
— AMOS 7:7-8

For who has despised the day of small things? For these seven rejoice to see the plumb line in the hand of Zerubbabel. They are the eyes of the LORD, which scan to and from throughout the whole earth.
—ZECHARIAH 4:10

As we function in our roles as kings and priests, we position ourselves for the plumb line to fall. When the angel of the Lord spoke to both Joshua and Zerubbabel, the plumb line *only* fell into the hand of Zerubbabel. The word tells us that the roles of the priests in prayer looks like a small thing but it facilitates the release of the plumb line into the hand of the kings. In other words, if you are not listening and watching in the place of prayer, you will not be available to receive the words that belong to you for your life, family, and purpose and bring you into the fullness of love.

The Lord spoke about this plumb line to two prophets in ancient Israel: Amos and Zechariah. Today, He is speaking to prophets again about this plumb line. The Holy Spirit told me to "Rebuild His Temple." Then showed me that He is rebuilding or bringing the capstone of Zerubbabel's temple. The Lord Himself appeared to Jeff Jansen and sent an angel to Steven Shelley to announce, "The plumb line is now in the hands of Zerubbabel." When God encounters multiple people in dramatic ways to declare a message to His Church, we need to pay attention.

This plumb line, then, is very important to the Lord. When the Lord says through His prophets that a "Cyrus" has been seated in the White House and the plumb line is now in the hands of Zerubbabel, we know that we are in the day that God is rebuilding Zerubbabel's temple which will house the Melchizedek priesthood. God is restoring order to His Church and rebuilding His priests; and when He constructs, He always uses a plumb line.

Therefore, I have dedicated three chapters to what I believe is revelation for the Church today. The Lord told Zerubbabel that the seven spirits of God rejoice to see the plumb line restored to the Church. Why is this such a big deal? What is the plumb line and why is it important?

As mentioned previously, and naturally speaking, a plumb line is a stone that hangs from a string that is used in construction of a building, home, etc. It is used to create a center of truth to determine a perpendicular line that measures everything against it. It is used in building the temple, or any building, both physical and spiritual. This is important since it is used to set the foundation in place and to begin the process of rebuilding or completing the work.

We see from the two chapter-opening Scriptures that the plumb line represents: 1) *a time of building;* and 2) *a time of judgment or realignment.* When you build a house, you have to clear the land of everything that will obstruct construction of the building. The Lord reveals Himself as the One who has the plumb line in His hand to tear down (Amos 9) and to build (Zechariah 4). How does God build and realign? With His Word.

The Plumb Line Is the Word of Truth

Prophetically, the plumb line is the *Word of Truth.* The Word became flesh and dwelt among us—Jesus. The Word was in the beginning and was God. *"All things were made through Him, and without Him nothing was made that was made"* (John 1:3). The plumb line is used first in construction and testing what is built, and second, in the work of destruction and tearing down what is not straight. After the foundation is laid with the plumb line, then the walls will be tested and built with this same plumb line before the capstone—in this case, the last generation—can be completed.

The temple of humankind is no different. We are built in Christ *not by power nor by might but by the Spirit of God.* Or as the writer of Hebrews tells us, this temple is not made by human hands but by a loving God (Hebrews 9:11). I speak in terms of individual and corporate work of the plumb line. The plumb line, which is the Word of Truth, will judge the hearts and minds of all people (Hebrews 4:12), the places where the law is now written (Hebrews 8:10). It separates between soul and spirit.

The plumb line that is in the hand of Zerubbabel is a measuring tool that will test how we are building our temples. Are we building according to the Word of Truth? The gold, silver, and precious stones speak to a life of prayer and obedience that is costly in time, money and even choosing love in the face of difficulty. The wood, hay, and straw are easily gained to build a house according to the wisdom of this age that will not stand. The Word will measure which building supplies you have used in your construction and the result will either be reward or loss and frustration.

> *For no other foundation can anyone lay than that which is laid, which is Jesus Christ. Now if anyone builds on this foundation with gold, silver, precious stones, wood, hay, straw, each one's work will become clear; for the Day will declare it, because it will be revealed by fire; and the fire will test each one's work, of what sort it is. If anyone's work which he has built on it endures, he will receive a reward. If anyone's work is burned, he will suffer loss; but*

he himself will be saved, yet so as through fire (1 Corinthians 3:11-15).

The plumb line aligns our methods of building with His. This frees us from the deception of humanism and human traditions that have crept into the Church and into the lives of God's priests. People use manipulation and control to build their ministries and their own kingdoms. But if we are going to build God's Kingdom, we have to do it His way. We need the plumb line. We need the Word of Truth. We only receive this plumb line when we take time in prayer to sit at His feet and listen to His words. Just like Mary, we have to choose the "good part" (Luke 10:42).

We will only return to our right minds, see clearly, and build properly when we are in full agreement with the Word of Truth. It is in this place of agreement where we truly are able to release His power and reveal His glory on the earth. His greatest desire is for us to rule and reign on the earth in partnership with Him.

In Luke 4:18, Jesus announced His mission. In the anointing of the Holy Spirit, He came to preach good news to the poor, to bind up the brokenhearted. He came to deliver us from the demonic oppression in our hearts and souls—mind, will, and emotions—to heal our bodies and open our spiritual eyes. This is His love at work in and through our hearts. In other words, Jesus came to make the crooked places straight, to align us with His heart. To free us from all deception and bondage to the enemy and empower us to become conduits for His words to be released.

As we pray, God releases His Word over us and removes the words of the enemy. He realigns us with His thoughts and His ways. His desire is to remove all flesh, motives, selfish ambitions, worldly thinking, and soul hurts that hinder the fullness of love and oneness with Him.

God's plumb line removes our ability to govern our lives through our emotions, our fears, our poverty mindsets, and our past trauma. He came to heal the human heart so that we could come into the fullness of love and fullness of joy. This is the Zechariah 3 experience where He purifies His priests, where we receive clean robes (right standing) and a clean turban (right thinking). His Word sets us apart as a holy priesthood (Zechariah 3), which prepares us to rule and reign with Him as kings (Zechariah 4). Once the land of our hearts has been cleared and the foundation leveled by His plumb line, He can begin the building. From here, He leads us into the Zechariah 4 "Shouts of Grace, grace," which I will cover in a later chapter. Fortunately, this is not a 12-step program but a dance of intimacy where His kindness leads us to repentance.

Your Story

The Bible tells us that God knew you before you were formed in your mother's womb and that He knows the beginning to the end. He has written every story of every person who has and is and will be born. He is the Author and Finisher of our story. Revelation tells us that at the end of the age God will open our book to see if our lives were lived according to His words.

And I saw the dead, small and great, standing before God, and books were opened. And another book was opened, which is the Book of Life. And the dead were judged according to their works, by the things which were written in the books (Revelation 20:12).

Since our stories have already been written in the Book of Life, He is looking for those who will trust His leadership and enter into His rest. We get fearful when we think we are going to experience loss and pain; but if we remain in prayer, we can hear His voice as He continues reading our story over us. This gives us the confidence and hope in His leadership in our lives because He works everything together for our good. Jesus is fully confident in Himself as the Word to lead us, transform us and partner with us to create our future.

The plumb line opens our eyes and ears. A great example of this plumb line revelation is the testimony of the two men walking on the road to Emmaus (Luke 24:13-31). They were dialoging and despondent about the death of Jesus, which is our similar condition when we look at our earthly circumstances without the perspective of heaven's words over us. Jesus Himself drew near and began to walk with the two men on the road to Emmaus. The Bible says that their eyes were "restrained," meaning they had eyes but could only see in the natural. Then Jesus began to speak; He told them about Himself, the Word in the Scriptures from Moses and all the prophets. Their eyes were awakened when they ate of the bread that He broke and blessed and they said, *"Did not our heart burn within us while He talked with us on the road, and while*

He opened the Scriptures to us?" (Luke 24:32). Jesus, the Living Word served as a plumb line to separate their souls—mind, will, and emotions—from their spirits, and it brought a burning into their hearts so they could be awakened to the truth.

The by-product of the cleansing of our hearts and minds is *the awakening of our ears to hear and our eyes to see what the Spirit of Truth is doing and saying.* This process brings us into the faith we need to bring the reality of the Kingdom into the earth. Let me take a moment to say that Jesus Christ completed and finished all at the cross. All the power, authority, and intimacy is available. However, most of His Church is still being held captive in their hearts and minds, without an understanding of how to access heaven and transform the earth.

Let me ask you a question, do you think the God of all the universe, who created the heavens and earth and all that is in it, sent His Son to the earth to die on the cross a brutal death, to rise on the third day, and to sit at the right hand of the Father so He could start a religion? Or do you believe the truth that He sent His Son to reconcile His family to Himself and to restore their true identity, the new creation as Christ-men and Christ-women, filled with the Spirit, living from the inside out, rooted in the Word, led by the Spirit? A new species who have become the temple of the living Word where we live awakened to His voice releasing a sound of heavens' thoughts, wisdom, and words. He speaks through us to transform the earth into His footstool and His garden.

The plumb line acts as a sword that cuts between soul and spirit. It measures where we are in our hearts. It tests our foundation, how straight the walls of our hearts and minds (temples) have become. Without the plumb line, we remain in confusion. It is both *Logos* and *Rhema* words—the written words of Scripture and the "now" words spoken to us by the Holy Spirit—that separate the things that are defiled and profane from the things that are holy and upright. The soul life is composed of the mind, will, and emotions.

When our *souls* do not line up with the Word of Truth (the plumb line), our *minds* will look at the facts in the natural, and we will judge and come up with a right or wrong conclusion based on what we see. Our *emotions* will get attached and assign motives to the actions of other people, to circumstances, and situations of life. This is typically motivated by fear. Our *will* succumbs to the influence of our mind and our emotions, and we become victims of life circumstances instead of overcomers in Christ. But we are called to live as ambassadors of heaven where the truth will trump the facts, the feelings we are experiencing, and the thoughts we are having must come under the authority of His words.

The plumb line serves as a judgment, a measurement of all things that are in relationship to it. Jesus said that He did not come to judge the world but to save it (John 3:17). But He also said that His Word will judge the world (John 12:48). Everything that is said and done will be judged, or *measured* against His Word to see if it is truth. He saves us by grace through faith (Ephesians 2:8), but we need His words to keep us in step with Him as we live our lives. The judgment of His Word keeps us within the safe boundaries of His will for our life. This enables us to be fruitful in our lives. *"If you abide in*

Me, and My words abide in you, you will ask what you desire, and it shall be done for you" (John 15:7).

In the first apostolic church, the plumb line (the Word of Truth) was readily available, leading them into all truth and laying the foundation of the faith with words from heaven. The Spirit was poured out and they *prophesied*. They spoke words of truth. They spoke words from heaven. They relied on the Spirit of Truth to speak to them and lead them.

However, many churches teach that God doesn't speak anymore. They accept the *Logos* dimension of the plumb line (the written Word, the Bible), but the *Rhema* dimension of the plumb line (the "now" word) is absent, which keeps their people in the confused state of darkness and wilderness living. In order to build properly, we must have both the *Logos* and the *Rhema*. You can look at the first church and their cooperation between the written and prophetic revelatory words and see that this is a guide of how to live. The *Logos* helps us to produce the fruit of the Spirit and the *Rhema* helps us directionally to be led by the Spirit.

Today, we see a reemergence of the plumb line with the increase of the apostles and prophets functioning in faith, hearing, seeing, and delivering the prophetic and gospel with power. This is how the foundation generation of the Church was built, and this is how the capstone generation will build.

12

THE PLUMB LINE CLEANSES THE PROPHETIC

We can see that the Lord has released His voice back to His people in this generation. I believe with His angelic announcement, "The plumb line is now in the hands of Zerubbabel," He is taking His priesthood beyond just the gifts of the Spirit. The plumb line cleans our minds and hearts so that the words of heaven come through priests with pure hearts.

We as the Church have struggled learning how to steward the prophetic. Some in the Church have been blessed by the prophetic and some have been hurt by those who have used or abused it. The brilliance of God to release a hunger and desire for prayer in our busy lives is His blueprint for His Word to return. He is beginning His work of restoration and bringing the capstone, final harvest. Those who say yes to a life of prayer will be those He uses in the future.

As I mentioned in the previous chapter, God is cleaning up His priesthood so they will have clean hands and pure hearts for the Word of God to flow through them without resistance or corruption.

As it was with the apostles at Pentecost, so it will be with those who will release His words now and in the future. Notice that the fire fell on those who were in one place, in one accord *praying*. When the Holy Spirit was poured out, it was for the purpose of the living Word through the prophetic being available again. This is why Peter gave the explanation of what was happening from Acts 2:17-18, that God poured out His Spirit on all flesh, both men and women *so they can prophesy!* The fire of God rested on and cleansed their minds so the word could flow through pure vessels, establishing a level foundation on which His Church was to be built.

Jesus said that even the least in the Kingdom, after Pentecost, would be greater prophets than John the Baptist.

Today, there has been a release of the gifts of the Spirit through the Charismatic Renewal of the 1960s and 1970s. The Church has embraced the gifts, and rightfully so; but in many ways it has forsaken the written Word and deemed it less than. We must be rooted in the Bible *and* led by the Spirit. If we leave the Word behind, we become the flaky, sinful prophets who may operate in the gifts of the Spirit with great power, but bring harm to the Church because we lack the fruits of the Spirit, the nature of God.

I have witnessed and experienced firsthand prophets whose hearts are not in accordance with God's plumb line of truth. As Jeremiah Johnson said, "Prophetic people who refuse community and accountability are dangerous and cannot be trusted." They often lack a consistent life in prayer, and have no humility and fear of the Lord. They operate as wolves among the sheep, using the prophetic for self-promotion and to build their own Kingdom. Many have been burned by the prophetic as a result, and so they are skeptical, suspicious, or even antagonistic toward the prophetic. But God said that when He pours out His Spirit, His people would prophesy. The right response to abuses of the prophetic is not to reject it, dismiss it, or diminish its value and necessity. Instead, we must encourage the Body of Christ to pray, connect to *the* Teacher, *the* Healer, *the* Counselor, and *the* Word.

The War of the Ages

I don't think I can talk about the prophetic being released without giving an understanding of the war of words. It is not a battle between people but between the words of God and the lying words of satan. I believe understanding this will help us to be wiser stewards of God's words in our generation.

The Bible tells us that the Word of God is referred to as the *seed*:

> *Now the parable is this: The seed is the word of God* (Luke 8:11).
>
> *Having been born again, not of corruptible seed but incorruptible, through the word of God which lives and abides forever* (1 Peter 1:23).

God tells us about this battle of this seed over His Word, in Genesis 1. So I am going to take you back to the beginning of time.

In the beginning God *spoke* the world into existence with four words: Let. There. Be. Light. His words formed the world. His words have creative power.

> *By faith we understand that the worlds were framed by the word of God, so that the things which are seen*

were not made of things which are visible (Hebrews 11:3).

Then in the process of the days of creation, God placed a universal principle that is an absolute in His Kingdom. This principle applies to all creation: every animal, thought, word, and deed. It applies to every tribe, tongue, nation both the lost and the saved. It is the creation of the seed:

> *...the herb that yields seed according to its kind, and the tree that yields fruit, whose seed is in itself according to its kind. And God saw that it was good* (Genesis 1:12).

The principle is this: *Every seed will reproduce after its own kind.*

So there was Adam and Eve, they were ruling and reigning the earth with God as His son and daughter. They were connected deeply in intimacy with God and with each other. But then the serpent came and *spoke words* that confused Eve and caused her to believe another story, another narrative/word other than what God spoke. The serpent tempted Eve by questioning the Word of God, "Has God indeed *said...?*"

The root etymology of the word *serpent* means "to hiss, to whisper divination or practice sorcery" (*nachash* -Gesenius' Hebrew-Chaldee Lexicon). So the serpent was *speaking words of witchcraft* that introduced confusion and trapped Eve into believing the words of creation over the words of the Creator. Therefore, God brought a curse on the serpent and put a battle between the seed of the serpent and the Seed of the woman.

I will put enmity between you and the woman, and between your seed and her Seed; He shall bruise your head, and you shall bruise His heel (Genesis 3:15).

This "seed" generally speaks to Eve's physical offspring. But it also speaks more specifically to Jesus, the Seed of Eve who would crush the head of satan. But Jesus is also called the Word who will defeat all darkness. The apostle John wrote in John 1:1-5:

In the beginning was the Word, and the Word was with God and the Word was God. He was in the beginning with God. All things were made through Him, and without Him nothing was made that was made. In Him was life, and the life was the light of men. And the light shines in the darkness, and the darkness did not comprehend it.

So Jesus, the Seed who would crush the head of the serpent is also the Word of life and light that wars against and overpowers the darkness.

So the battle of the ages is over the Word. There is a battle between the word of divination (or confusion) and the Word of God. The promise, however, is that this battle will be won because the blood of Jesus "speaks" a better word than that of the serpent. The Seed or the Word will strike satan's head, but the serpent's words will bruise the heel of the Word. This means that while the words of the enemy can cause us to stumble, the words of Christ will destroy the serpent's words that are being spoken to your mind. The living Word will subjugate the words of the enemy.

Remember that every word will reproduce after itself and this includes the words of satan. The words of demons have power because of the principle of reproduction that God put in the universe. When Jesus came, He tore the veil between heaven and earth so the plumb line (the Word of Truth) could come to rebuild His living temples according to His will. So His Seed could be reproduced on earth.

We must learn to war as Jesus did. John the Baptist prophesied over Jesus, saying, *"Behold! The Lamb of God who takes away the sins of the world!"* (John 1:29). After he baptized Jesus and the Spirit descended as a dove, the promise of "You are My beloved Son" was released. *He received the Word of Truth over His life.* Immediately Jesus *was tested* over the Word concerning His Sonship and authority. The Spirit led Him into the wilderness, and the enemy met Him to challenge the word saying, *"If You are the Son of God..."* (Luke 4:3). The very words that God just released over Him were tested. In the wilderness the enemy had not bothered Jesus before that time, but when the plumb line fell containing the seeds of truth, it activated the battle. But how did Jesus respond? *With the Word, the Scriptures.*

> But Jesus answered him, saying, "It is written, 'Man shall not live by bread alone, but by every word of God'" (Luke 4:4).

Jesus responded to the word of the accuser with the Word of the Lord. When we are confronted with the words of the enemy, with the words of what we are seeing with our natural eyes, we must respond with the Word of the Lord. But notice that Jesus not only responded in the moment of trial with the Word of God. He *lived* by the Word of God. We must live not by natural bread alone but by the bread that came down from heaven, the words of life from heaven, and were recorded in the Bible, the inspired Word of God.

We cannot only speak out the Word of God when circumstances get difficult. We need the daily bread of God's Word. We must daily feed on the Word of God and let it richly dwell in our hearts (Colossians 3:16), so that when the testing comes we are ready to release it from our mouths. Whatever words we feed on daily, those words we store in the soil of our hearts. Whatever words we store in our hearts reproduce themselves, and *those* words will come out of our mouths, from our hearts, during the time of testing. "*...For out of the abundance of the heart the mouth speaks*" (Matthew 12:34).

The Word of the Lord was absolutely key in the building of Zerubbabel's temple. The enemies of Israel were releasing words of discouragement and words of death so that the people of God would stop building. But the Word of the Lord came through Haggai and Zechariah. God provided His Word to Zerubbabel; and even in the midst of opposition, the completion of the temple came through shouts (words) of "Grace, grace." Keeping the words of the Lord in our hearts and releasing them during trial and testing are necessary to building not by might nor by power, but by His Spirit.

13

THE COMING SOUND WITH SHOUTS OF GRACE

There is a sound coming and it is the sound of the Son within us. He is awakening us to release His words in power. These words are available to the awakened ones. As you learn to work the word, the word will work for you.

—TRACY ECKERT

The Father is bringing His finishing work through this capstone generation. He is bringing it forth with a double measure of grace on our shouts (sound), prophecies, songs, words, and declarations. Everything in your life in the Kingdom is built up or torn down through words. His Word is alive and being given more grace than at any other time in the history of the Church.

As I have said in the last couple of chapters, God is releasing His plumb line to clean up the hearts and minds of His priests so they can be used to complete the building of His Kingdom age by anointing their words. William Branham, who was the father of the latter rain healing revival, prophesied about this generation through Buford Dowell before his death saying:

> God is going to take every move of God that we have heard of in history and even what we witnessed in Bible days and put it all together in one big Holy Ghost bomb and drop it on earth. The nations will reel with the power of God like they have never seen and prime time news will cover it. God is going to bring the ministry of the apostles and prophets to the forefront. They will have the mind of God, the heart of God and the voice of God and when they speak, their words will be the words of God. They won't just speak about the future, they will create realities with God. Whatever they say, God will create it because it will be His mind, His will, and His word. It won't be about them, it will be about Him.[1]

We will create the future with God. As we function in the branches of government ordained by God as priests and kings before Him, we will rule and reign in the earth fully aligned with heaven's words.

In Ephesians 4, Paul says that the Church is being given the fivefold ministry *until* there is unity of the faith that will facilitate the perfection of humankind.

> *Until we all reach unity in the faith and in the knowledge of the Son of God and become mature, attaining to the whole measure of the fullness of*

> *Christ....Instead, speaking the truth in love, we will grow to become in every respect the mature body of him who is the head, that is, Christ* (Ephesians 4:13,15 NIV).

I believe this speaks of the same unity Jesus spoke of in John 17:21, that we would be one with Him and the Father: *"that they all may be one, as You, Father, are in Me, and I in You; that they also may be one in Us, that the world may believe that You sent Me."*

Again, this perfection of humanity is mentioned by James in connection to the words that we speak that control our whole body, the trajectory of our lives as a rudder deciding our future that will either be decided by God, or by the enemy.

> *We all stumble in many ways. Anyone who is never at fault in what they say is perfect, able to keep their whole body in check* (James 3:2 NIV).

While prophecy is becoming more acceptable in the Body of Christ, most people do not understand how to work the word that is given so that the word works to create momentum and prosperity in their lives. They receive a prophetic word that encourages them and makes them feel good and it gives them hope. All of this is good. However, the words are supposed to be used as a sword to create, establish, and tear down.

Most of the Body of Christ, even in Charismatic circles, live as wilderness wanderers and are fed morsels of manna (prophetic words) from God, because He is good to supply our hearts with His living Word. However, the word is given so we can speak and create the beautiful and joyful life waiting for us where we can have the abundance of living in the reality of our created purpose. The bread from heaven, the Living Word has come.

Becoming One With the Word

Jesus is returning for a bride who is His image bearer. The new priesthood of both priest and king is the only way for us to be in union with God and the exact representation of Jesus. We will look like Him, meaning we have become one with His Word. In the book of Hebrews, it says that faith in His Word produces a substance that helps to facilitate the production of what we are believing God for. The Greek word *substance* is *hypostasis,* which basically means that faith is the foundation that has actual existence. This substance is where the Word of God becomes one with us.

> *Faith is the substance of things hoped for, the evidence of things not seen* (Hebrews 11:1).

Faith has substance but so does fear. Faith *activates* the word—fear or unbelief *stops* the Word. This substance is the enabling element that creates union with the Word. The theological term "hypostatic union," which is derived from the word *substance* (hypostasis), was used at the Council of Chalcedon in AD 451. It describes the union of the divine nature and human nature in the person of Jesus Christ. It speaks of how the divine Word has become *one* with human flesh.

Now, this is a unique term that specifically applies to Jesus, the Eternal Son of God; but there's a powerful analogy I want to make here between this and what happens to us when we have faith. When we believe the words or promises God has spoken to us, His words start to dwell, or abide, inside us; and through His words and promises, we share in His divine nature. His words, which are spirit and life, strengthen us because His divine life flows through them. This causes a new place of intimacy and authority in prayer.

> *Grace and peace be multiplied to you in the knowledge of God and of Jesus our Lord, as His divine power has given to us all things that pertain to life and godliness, through the knowledge of Him who called us by glory and virtue, by which have been given to us exceedingly great and precious promises, that through these you may be partakers of the divine nature, having escaped the corruption that is in the world through lust* (2 Peter 1:2-4).
>
> *If you abide in Me, and My words abide in you, you will ask what you desire, and it shall be done for you. By this My Father is glorified, that you bear much fruit; so you will be My disciples* (John 15:7-8).

This is what Paul was talking to the Ephesians about when he wrote that the fivefold ministry would be given to the Church for a time, but there would come a generation that would mature beyond this in their identity as priest and king with Christ as the Head. This becoming *one* with the Word or *unity of the faith* creates the substance of answered prayers and authority to create the future with God (Ephesians 4:13,15).

Paul writes of this same reality when he references Abraham's faith that was the substance that enabled Sarah to give birth to Isaac when it was physically impossible. He was fully convinced in God's Word and God's ability to supernaturally perform His promise; therefore, it was accounted to him for righteousness. The Word says that God answers the prayers of righteous people. The righteousness comes as a by-product of us being fully convinced and in agreement with God's Word and ways.

> He [Abraham] *did not waver at the promise of God through unbelief, but was strengthened in faith, giving glory to God and being fully convinced that what He had promised He was also able to perform* (Romans 4:20-21).

Jesus demonstrated the very productive life of the priestly and kingly order of Melchizedek. As we walk in this same order, it achieves the fullness of the stature of Christ within us. We become fully who we were created by God to be with our gifts, personalities, and callings functioning, allowing the fullness of God's glory to radiate from us.

God told Mike Bickle that He was changing the expression of Christianity in one generation. When we started the HOZ (House of Zerubbabel, that we renamed Storehouse), the Lord told me that this was not His house of prayer, the *people* were His houses of prayer. The rebuilt Tabernacle of David is not just a prayer room but a body prepared for His habitation.

The Lord in His great providence and knowledge awakened the priesthood through the prayer movement in these houses of prayer; but that is not His end game or the expression of Christianity that He is after. If we leave it there, then the Great Commission and the fullness of His government and glory will not be seen rising in us.

Dream of Luke 4:18

I saw the Lord's finger point to Luke 4:18 in the Bible and heard Him say, "It was Luke 4:18 but now Isaiah 61." As I have said previously, Jesus came to first clean up His priests which He proclaimed in Luke 4:18 so we can function in the fullness of the Melchizedek priesthood as kings, which He demonstrated throughout His ministry.

> *The Spirit of the LORD is upon Me, because He has anointed Me to preach the gospel to the poor; He has sent Me to heal the brokenhearted, to proclaim liberty to the captives and recovery of sight to the blind, to set at liberty those who are oppressed* (Luke 4:18).

In this passage, Jesus proclaimed His mission statement while standing in the synagogue. In Luke 4:18 Jesus is quoting the first part of Isaiah 61. The rest of Isaiah 61 in verses 3-11 is the result of His cleanup operation, His effective, strong, prosperous, and holy priesthood. This priesthood will rebuild old ruins, raise up former desolations (barrenness), and repair ruined cities from generations of captivity. We will eat the riches of the wicked, receive double honor, and live with understanding of the system of the Kingdom. We will be known as priests of the Lord and our children shall be blessed. This is your Promised Land.

> To console those who mourn in Zion, to give them beauty for ashes, the oil of joy for mourning, the garment of praise for the spirit of heaviness; that they may be called trees of righteousness, the planting of the LORD, that He may be glorified.
>
> And they shall rebuild the old ruins, they shall raise up the former desolations, and they shall repair the ruined cities, the desolations of many generations. Strangers shall stand and feed your flocks, and the sons of the foreigner shall be your plowmen and your vinedressers. But you shall be named the priests of the LORD, they shall call you the servants of our God. You shall eat the riches of the Gentiles, and in their glory you shall boast. Instead of your shame you shall have double honor, and instead of confusion they shall rejoice in their portion. Therefore in their land they shall possess double; everlasting joy shall be theirs.
>
> For I, the LORD, love justice; I hate robbery for burnt offering; I will direct their work in truth, and will make with them an everlasting covenant. Their descendants shall be known among the Gentiles, and their offspring among the people. All who see them shall acknowledge them, that they are the posterity whom the LORD has blessed.

I will greatly rejoice in the LORD, my soul shall be joyful in my God; for He has clothed me with the garments of salvation, He has covered me with the robe of righteousness, as a bridegroom decks himself with ornaments, and as a bride adorns herself with her jewels. For as the earth brings forth its bud, as the garden causes the things that are sown in it to spring forth, so the Lord GOD will cause righteousness and praise to spring forth before all the nations (Isaiah 61:3-11).

If you take inventory of the promises that await this kind of priesthood, you will run to the place of prayer. We all know intuitively that this is our inheritance in Christ, but we haven't known how to build this kind of life.

How to Build

The priestly order of Melchizedek knows how to get the sound from heaven to earth. The how-to is located in First John 5:7-15.

John tells us that there are three in heaven: *"the Father, the Word, and the Holy Spirit."* It is interesting that He does not say the Father, the Son, and the Holy Spirit. He is trying to make the point of how to get Jesus as the Word from heaven to earth. We have the description of what is happening in heaven: the Father, the Word, and the Holy Spirit *are One.* The Father, the Word, and the Spirit speaking in perfect unity. They are bearing witness, which means there is a testimony being proclaimed in heaven. Revelation 19:10 tells us that the testimony of Jesus, in heaven, is the spirit of prophecy. Therefore, we can conclude that heaven is prophesying. Heaven has something to say to us.

On earth, there is a similar yet different situation. There are also *three who bear witness on earth*: the Spirit, the water, and the blood and these three *agree as One*. The water and blood are defined earlier in First John 5:6, *"This is He who came by water and blood—Jesus Christ; not only by water, but by water and blood. And it is the Spirit who bears witness, because the Spirit is truth."*

This is the same blood and water that happens during childbirth. When the side of Adam was pierced and a rib removed, he gave birth to his bride, Eve. Again, when the side of Jesus was pierced, out flowed water and blood, giving birth to His bride, you and me. We are Christ-women and Christ-men.

So we have Jesus Christ, the oily One, the Anointed One, living inside us and "the Spirit who bears witness to the truth" (1 John 5:6). This gives us access to what the Three in heaven are saying. The following diagram illustrates how we receive the words of heaven so we can release them into the earth.

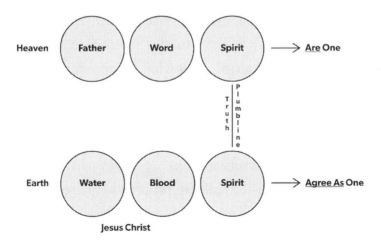

As you can see in the diagram, the Three in heaven *are* One. However, on earth, *there is an activity required of us.*

- We receive.
- We believe.
- We declare.

We must 1) *receive* what heaven is saying; we must receive the Word of Truth by the Holy Spirit, who is Truth. Then we must 2) *believe* and be "fully convinced" as Abraham was when he received the word of the Lord (Romans 4:21). In other words, we must be in full agreement with the words of God, no matter what we see in front of us. When we hear and see what heaven is saying and doing and we *agree* in our hearts with His words which are *truth,* we 3) declare this *truth* out of our mouths and into the earth, and then creation must respond. Through this process that God set up in the beginning, we function in the order of Melchizedek. John the beloved goes on in First John 5:14-15 to say:

> *Now this is the confidence that we have in Him, that if we ask anything according to His will [words], He hears us. And if we know that He hears us, whatever we ask, we know that we have the petitions that we have asked of Him.*

If we want effective prayer, prayer that actually shifts and changes our lives and in the earth, we must ask "according to His will." According to the Word of heaven. How do I know the will of God? I am going to spend more time on this in the next chapter with some testimonies. But it boils down to this

Melchizedek priesthood. We come into the presence of God as priests. We worship, give thanks, and offer up our petitions. In that place our ears become opened to the Spirit of Truth, who is in full agreement with the Father and the Word. We receive the plumb line—His will, His words, His Truth, and we agree with them. Then, as kings we declare them out loud, fully convinced that "we have the petitions that we have asked of Him."

This is the sound that resounds from heaven—the truth, the plummet stone (plumb line). The truth, His Word is dropped from heaven into the human temple not made with hands, measuring how straight the lines are within the walls of our hearts and giving us hope and a future. It is measuring what we believe and how big Christ is in us. I recently had a dream where I was given a machine that measured Christ in me by measuring how much light I have within me. Our destiny is Galatians 2:20, "*...it is no longer I who live, but Christ lives in me; and the life which I now live in the flesh, I live by faith in the Son of God...*"

When the word comes, will you receive and believe and agree? Or will you say God's word is often different from what we see with our natural eyes.

Jesus told the Pharisees in John 5:39-40, "*You search the Scriptures, for in them you think you have eternal life; and these are they which testify of Me. But you are not willing to come to Me that you may have life.*" It is *prophecy*—the word of the Lord—released into the earth that declares the truth that trumps the lies of the enemy. It brings down every word that is raised up against His righteous ones. It creates, it establishes, it builds up and tears down. Through His Word, Christ still lives and is co-creating with His holy ones. This is rulership, this is dominion with Christ.

To be clear, the Scripture is certainly important. The Bible is indeed the Word of God. It is God-breathed, and everything we hear personally from the Lord must be grounded and measured by the Scriptures. Otherwise we risk running off into heresy. Sometimes people get the idea that prophecy and hearing from God personally can replace the need to search the Bible. This is not what I am saying.

We are called to know the Scriptures, to teach the Scriptures, and apply the Scriptures.

> *All Scripture is given by inspiration of God, and is profitable for doctrine, for reproof, for correction, for instruction in righteousness, that the man of God may be complete, thoroughly equipped for every good work* (2 Timothy 3:16-17).

However, Jesus says that is possible to diligently study the Scriptures, the written Word, yet not actually come to the Living Word. The Pharisees and scribes knew the Scriptures very well, but they didn't come to the One about whom the Scriptures testify. The Lord wants us to come into His presence, to sit at His feet and hear the words from His own mouth. To receive the words of the Three in heaven (the Father, the Word, and the Spirit) and to be in full unity and agreement with them.

Three Are Coming Together as One

I heard the Lord say to me, "THE THREE ARE COMING TOGETHER AS ONE. DID YOU THINK I WOULDN'T GIVE THIS TO YOU?" I thought it was strange because I thought, *Wait, the Three are One.* But He was speaking about the unity of the faith. Again, this is the *unity of the faith* that Paul was describing in Ephesians 4:13: *"till we all come to the unity of the faith and of the knowledge of the Son of God, to a perfect man, to the measure of the stature of the fullness of Christ."*

The Three coming together, agreeing as One, and prophesying what we hear and see, fully releasing heaven's reality on the earth, will bring the earth into submission so that heaven will release Jesus to return back home. But for now, *He must remain in heaven until the time for the final restoration of all things, as God promised long ago through His holy prophets* (Acts 3:21).

When I hear from heaven and I speak the word that I hear, it creates faith in me; and through agreement, I have become one with the word. The Word and the flesh have become One creating the substance that makes what I say happen. This is the *union of the faith* or the *Three coming together as One.*

Four Ways to Live in Unity of the Faith

1. ***Pray as priests*** to access words and pictures.
2. ***Speak as kings*** His words and follow His commands.

3. *Faith* to believe and agree with His words or commands.

4. *Patience* to endure, overcome, and stand on the word when we have to wait for the fulfillment of the promise of what He promised.

The Word of God isn't just a bunch of stories in a book. The Bible isn't just principles to live by. The Word of God isn't just a list of do's and don'ts. The Word of God is living and active. It is creative and anointed and is supposed to be one with us.

Testimonies—Applying the Plumb Line

As we sit before the feet of Jesus and minister to Him, we hear His words of life. At this point we have a decision to make. Do we believe or reject His words? We are created for love and for truth, not fear and lies. When we elevate facts (stating obvious conditions that are present) over God's prophetic words, we are choosing to live in the earth's cursed system. We can see facts with our natural eyes.

Remember, there are two trees in the garden. As believers, we are supposed to be *seeking* and *believing* the words of life. This is where we are tested. The words of knowledge from the tree of good and evil will lead us down the wrong path. These are words that state the facts of what we see and know. This is not just knowledge of evil but also knowledge of good.

What happens when the God of heaven tells you to do something that looks the opposite of what the world says is good? What if He tells you to give away all your money when you have bills to pay? What if He tells you that your promise is in the land of giants? Every time the Lord promoted my husband, John, and I, it came at the cost of our natural inclination. Things that the world doesn't understand.

When John started his business, it took time to get it off the ground. We had gone through all our savings except one hundred dollars. We prayed and the Lord said to give away the last of what we had. This was so hard because we had six children to feed and bills to pay. In great pain and torment, we wrote the check and gave it away. Two days later, the Lord broke into John's business with a job that paid that week for $7,000.

Another time, the Lord had promised us a house and asked us to make a list of what we wanted. We had our list of all the amenities that we wanted in a home for our family. At that time, we had seven children and ten grandchildren, so we needed a large home and wanted to have some land. We had been saving for a down payment to buy our house for nine years. We had saved $7,000 over nine years, but we needed a $20,000 deposit for the house that was on our list. At the rate we were going, it would be another ten years before we could afford to buy our house.

One day I heard the Lord tell me to give away our house money to a couple in our church. I had a lot of emotion and longing attached to the promise of owning a home of my own. I could plant a garden, host friends, decorate. You know what I'm saying. It was my promise from the Lord. His command to give away my house money didn't make sense to the knowledge of what I know is good. We had worked hard to save that money.

Yet, I know that God is better than what I know is good. He is good, and I know that He knows more than I do. His ways are not my ways. His words and ways are higher than what I know and believe. This was a test of what I was going to believe. God or me?

John and I prayed, and we gave the money away. All $7,000. We sowed the money as God had commanded. We believed His truth over our knowledge of what is good. I'm not saying it was easy. Why would we give away the money that would bring in our promise?

A couple months later, I began packing up our things in boxes to move. I told John that we are moving. I believed that, even though we had given the entire $7,000 away, none of which had been replenished by the way. John, a little confused at why I was packing, said to me that it would take years to save the money we needed to buy a house. But I felt movement in the Spirit and I began to *declare out loud* that we were moving. I had a knowing that something was coming.

One month later, John got a surprise check in the mail of $21,000 from a business deal. Enough for us to buy a house! The next day we found our house that had everything on our list and bought it. The Lord was fulfilling His promise to us through supernatural and impossible means. When He commands it, we must respond even if it tests our natural understanding of how and what we believe. God is always in the business of promotion, multiplication, and dominion.

Let's review that promise for a minute. The "good" thing to do seemed to be to keep adding money to the $7,000 savings for our house. But God said *to give it away* and *believe* for our house. Once we did, the "facts" said it would take years to have enough money for the house. But the words of heaven in my spirit said, "You're moving. Start packing." So I *declared the word aloud* and *obeyed*. Two months later, we received the money, found our house, and moved in.

The words from heaven had to be seen and heard—*received*—with my spiritual eyes. Then it was my job to take dominion by fully *believing* what I saw and heard from heaven more than what I saw and heard on earth. Then I had to speak the *truth* of God's words over the lie in the factual, natural, earthly reality. God's words spoken through His priests will take dominion over every circumstance that the natural order presents. God's words are higher than words from the enemy and from conditions we see in the natural.

Another example of the Word of God over the facts on earth is a trip my family recently took to Costa Rica. We arrived to find out that we were visiting during the rainy season and the weather reports showed thunderstorms every day, *all* day. Well, those were the facts. Several people in our family stated the obvious, the facts, "It's going to rain every day because that is what the weather report says." But there is a higher truth. I said, "No, that is not the truth. Let's pray."

So I *asked* the Lord if I could change the weather for our vacation. Then I *saw* a picture of the sun and I knew I had my answer. So I called some of my intercessor friends and I *spoke* to the clouds and commanded no rain in our area. During the seven days we were there, it only rained for three hours. What did I do? I *asked* the Lord for the word of heaven. I *received* it in a vision and *believed* it. Then I *spoke* it out loud in faith in agreement with my intercessors. The Lord spoke to me (as a priest) and I spoke His word out loud (as a king).

The night before we left, our waiter at the resort commented on how weird the weather had been considering it was their rainy season. He said that the thunderclouds were all around the resort but the resort itself had clear skies all week. He didn't know that one of God's priests was staying at his resort.

These are but a couple of testimonies of the fruit of applying this lifestyle as priests and kings.

When Jesus, in the order of Melchizedek, was in the boat with His disciples and the violent storm arose, that was a fact; but the Word of Truth was in the boat and released His truth, calming the storm. Jesus lives in us. So if Jesus can calm the storm, so can we. If Jesus can heal the sick, so can we. If Jesus can prophesy, so can we. Because He lives in us. If we believe in Him, the Word, the Truth, we will do what He did and greater:

> *Most assuredly, I say to you, he who believes in Me, the works that I do he will do also; and greater works than these he will do, because I go to My Father* (John 14:12).

We can function in this level of kingly power, the greater works, but *only* if we are willing to function in this order of priesthood. This priesthood is rightly aligned between heaven and earth.

Therefore, we hear, we speak, we see, we act, and watch heaven's words change the earth and our lives.

We are the image bearers of the Father, Jesus the Word, and the Spirit when we function in the priesthood that Jesus died to bring to us. This is our identity, our new song, the hope of Christ in us fully aligned in movement, rhythm, and sound. He is rebuilding Zerubbabel's temple—Christ dwelling in humans—and completing the work of His house with shouts of "Grace! Grace!" in this hour. As we connect in prayer, yield to His leadership, and release His words back to Him and into the earth, we will see our prayers answered, and see the righteous no longer forsaken in the lives of our family, communities, cities, and the nations.

Endnote

1. Buford Dowell Testimony; https://www.youtube.com/watch?v=EjYqoTZqpcY, accessed July 24, 2020.

14

ACCESS HEAVEN — TRANSFORM EARTH

The emerging priesthood will believe more of what they don't see than what they do see. They will be faith champions who see and hear in the Spirit with understanding. They will run and not grow weary. Their shining will be because they have completely surrendered their lives, trusting and believing the Word of God over every lie of the enemy. They will give themselves to lives of abiding in prayer and adoration, then overcoming with declarations of the living Word. There will be no guile in them. They will have eyes set on their beloved Jesus.

We are the living tabernacle of Christ in us that Zerubbabel's temple signifies. Jesus is our Master Builder. Our High Priest and King in the Order of Melchizedek. He laid the foundation of His temple of God in humanity at Pentecost, remaking His people into His image as the shining lampstand, the light of the world, full of the golden oil of the Holy Spirit. This golden oil flowed from the two olive branches, the offices of king and priest. The first-century Church received the plumb line, the Word of Truth, the words from heaven, and released them into the earth.

Though the building of this living temple was frustrated and interrupted as the Church was corrupted with the wisdom of the world and human traditions, God is leading His people out of this confusion and into our inheritance. He has raised up prophets to declare that it's time to *rebuild His temple.*

Jesus is training this capstone generation, the generation that will usher in His return, to live in this king and priest lifestyle. He is completing His temple, bringing us into the unity of the faith, one with His Word, with shouts of "Grace! Grace!" No mountain, no obstacle to this level of maturity and unity will stand before us. Not by might, nor by power, but by His Spirit.

My journey has been interesting, to say the least. In the initial dream about starting a house of prayer, God told me, "If you teach them to pray, you don't have to tell them how to live." The cry of my heart is, "Lord, teach me to pray." God wants to awaken us with a One Thing desire, to have an intimate and vulnerable connection with Him and to give us the dreams and desires of our hearts. The promises that we know belong to us, but have never completely come in.

Personally, I was sick in my heart of wandering in the wilderness, and I knew there was a truth that was available. If God is saying that He answers the prayers of the righteous, then how can I find the key to unlock this mystery? Jesus said to seek His Kingdom way, and we would find the key to answered prayer so we can bring Him glory.

> But seek first the kingdom of God and His righteousness [His ways], *and all these things shall be added to you* (Matthew 6:33).

I was praying almost twenty hours a week in our house of prayer but still not seeing the type of victory that I knew I was supposed to have. I had fasted and contended, shouted, fasted some more for years, but still with limited breakthrough. I went away on a sabbatical and sought the Lord about prayer. He met me there and shared with me the most simple and profound truth about heaven's distribution process. He told me that His greatest desire is for His Bride to make herself ready, but she is too busy for Him. He is waiting for us, not the other way around. He wants to see us come into the fullness of our roles as kings and priests so He can pour out His glory.

In this chapter, I hope to make this concept of the king and priest more practical. This is how the Lord has been teaching me, and I have rarely seen my prayers unanswered. As I began to operate in the governmental authority that Jesus modeled, I was shocked and amazed at the fulfillment of my prayers. This is the King in a Kingdom who does not disappoint. I pray the testimonies of breakthrough in this chapter will fill you with faith for the impossible. These are only a few of the hundreds of answered prayers that are miraculous.

First, I am not out there praying for anything that He has not initiated. I only ask for what He has spoken to me. The more submitted I have become, the more I see answered prayers. I sought after His will for my life and began to ask for the details for every decision. You may think I am being obsessive, but I have learned the hard way that it's easier and more productive to ask first rather than have to repent and stall the forward momentum and then deal with the clean-up.

He told me to make a list of thankfulness and break it down into three categories:

1. Who He is to me
2. What He has promised me in Scripture
3. What He has promised me in prophecy

This was the Lord tutoring me. Even though I had clocked thousands of hours in prayer, I didn't know or understand how to use what I was hearing. It was like receiving an inheritance but not knowing how to invest it. As I mentioned before in Chapter 9, the parables teach us about the priest and king lifestyle in Matthew 25 of the *wise virgins* who gave themselves to intimacy and adoration of Jesus in prayer and the *investors of the talents.* I knew how to pray and love on Jesus, but I didn't understand what to do with what I heard and saw.

After a while, this will renew your mind and spirit. You will begin to naturally flow in the word and become adept at believing and declaring. In the beginning, I didn't believe, but I declared. The more I spoke His Word out loud over myself, the more convinced I became of its truth. My mind had to be transformed to believe and partner in that truth so I could see it happen on the earth. As I said in Chapter 13, our part is agreement or faith. The more my mind was renewed, I was fully convinced about His promises for me. I could see them happening. The substance of these things that were hoped for manifested as absolutes in the spirit and in my mind before I saw them happen in the natural.

Our heavenly encounters through dreams, visions, prophecies and hearing His voice are not for our entertainment or so that we feel good and important—it is for building up and tearing down, advancing His Kingdom, and destroying the works of darkness. These words are the sword of the Lord, the truth of God to be used to make earth like heaven. Once I learned how to invest His words through speaking and doing what I was hearing and seeing, I began to see a huge return on His investment in my life. Of course, this is all revealed in His Word, the Bible, but I never saw it like this. This simple, practical way of living out my role as a priest and a king has led to victory in my family life, my community, my region, and in the nations.

The following are a few samples of my written declarations that I speak *out loud*. I speak them out loud because scientists have discovered that your own voice has more power over your mind than any voice. It can change the inner pathways of your brain. I speak Scripture out loud over myself to prophesy the truth of heaven's words; and as I said, it also renews my mind. You want to begin with praise for who God is to you. Then I put all His biblical and prophetic promises in thankfulness. This is a sample; you can use your own words or choose Scripture to declare back to Him the truth of who He is. It is going through His gates with thanksgiving and His courts with praise (Psalm 100).

You can use any of these, but the third section of prophetic promises will have to be your own.

1. Who He is to me: Father, You are holy and Your name is holy. You are the One and Only True God. You are faithful and Your Word is true and eternal. You are worthy to receive wisdom, power, glory, riches, honor, strength, and glory. You

are Creator of heaven and earth and all that is in it. Father, I receive Your word. I pray for the peace and salvation of Israel.

2. What He has promised me in Scripture: Father, thank You that You uphold me according to Your promise, that I may live, and let me not be put to shame in my hope (Psalm 119:116). Father, thank You that my alms and prayers come up for a memorial before You (Acts 10:4). It is no longer I who lives but Christ who lives in me; and the life which I now live in the flesh, I live by the faith of the Son of God (Galatians 2:20). Father, thank You that I will rebuild Your temple and be filled with Your glory—not by might nor by power but by Your Spirit and all obstacles before me shall come down through Your grace (Zechariah 4, Haggai 2:6-9).

This is one of my favorites: Father, thank You that I fear the Lord and walk in Your ways and eat the labor of my hands and it will be well with me. Thank You that I am a fruitful vine in the very heart of my husband's house, and my children will be anointed and serve You (Psalm 128:1-4).

3. What He has promised me in prophecy: (Fill in your personal prophecies.)

I have seen tremendous supernatural fulfillments through listening and speaking, seeing and obeying. The following are a few testimonies:

Community—Victory Over Death

The Lord not only wants us to have victory in our personal lives, but in our community. A few years ago, I received a call from one of our staff from our house of prayer announcing that the husband of one of our worship leaders was being taken to the ER. He had fallen asleep in his truck and it was over 100 degrees outside. His body temperature spiked and he had suffered severe hyperthermia. He was in a coma, had coded several times, and his organs were shutting down. The doctors were saying that he was in a vegetative state. Even if he lived, he would never recover because of the organ and brain damage.

While he did not attend our house of prayer, his wife was a beloved family member, and they had a beautiful four-year-old daughter. I was so upset, really angry about this. I began to pray, asking the Lord what He was going to do about this. He said to me, "What are you going to do about this?"

I said to Him, "I don't know, what *am* I going to do about this?"

He said, "I want you to call a three-day fast, get everyone praying 24/7 for three days and go to the hospital, lay hands on him, and tell him that he will wake up in three days."

I called our house of prayer to a three-day fast and people helped develop an online prayer schedule where people could sign up for two-hour prayer sets. We developed a list of Scriptures that they could pray so we would be in one accord. We connected with his church community and many of his friends and coworkers jumped onboard and volunteered to pray and fast. I was so excited about the love and commitment by all who said yes.

I went to the hospital and walked through a large crowd of many of his closest friends who were there in the waiting room and hallway. I was so scared as I walked down the hall toward the ICU. I would like to tell you that I was this big faith champion. I finally got to his hospital bed where I went in alone, laid hands on him and said, "In three days you will wake up."

Three days later, he woke up with no brain or organ damage. The doctors declared his recovery a miracle. Once again, I sought the Lord for *heaven's words*. I *received, believed,* and *obeyed* the word of the Lord no matter what I saw, no matter what I felt. I *spoke His words aloud*—this is very important. God has a plan to restore what the enemy has stolen. All we have to do is be part of His plan. As priests we hear, and as kings we declare (out loud) and obey His Word. I followed the words that I heard even though it was impossible.

Will you be a priest in this hour who will cultivate a life in prayer so you can raise the dead? The words of life will bring down the facts of death, sickness. Who will go to heaven and get these words of Truth so things on earth will look like heaven? We should be known in our communities as a resource for the impossible. Individually and corporately, we should be known as the place where the supernatural is common, where wisdom comes from heaven, where people can learn to access heaven and transform earth. We are called to be a place where people come all the time with their last-resort cases, where they get healed and see that God is real. This is how Jesus, our High Priest and King, lived. He heard what His Father was saying and lived by *those* words. This is how He trained His disciples to live. This is how He is training His Church today to live.

Region—Victory Over Sex Trafficking

As the Church began to embrace this lifestyle as priests and kings, we became vessels of transformation in our region. In 2011, Dallas was chosen to host the Super Bowl. While this was exciting for our city, I was told the most terrifying statistics of the what happens with prostitution when a major sporting event comes to a city. Women and children are sex trafficked into the city leading up to the event, and the city becomes like a type of brothel for all who come to party before the game. The spike in prostitution remains at that level after the game is over and the city is left with the residue of this crime. When I heard this, again, I was so angry.

I have four beautiful daughters, and this was a justice issue that went all the way to the core of my heart. I was then and am today a huge advocate for rescuing these precious women and girls out of the abominable prison of sexual slavery. I believe this is a church issue first and a law enforcement issue second. I had this righteous indignation and my cry to the Lord and to others was "Not on my watch and not in my city." So I prayed and asked the Lord what He was going to do about this? And like usual, He said to me, "What are *you* going to do about this?"

I said, "I don't know. What *am* I going to do about this?"

He told me to call a 21-day fast, and hold a 3-day, 24-hour prayer and worship vigil the weekend before the events began. We got the word out to all the other churches, houses of prayer, and anti-sex trafficking organizations to join us. God gave His words to declare over Dallas and we were in one accord.

The weekend before the Super Bowl, we began our 24-hour time of prayer and worship. However, it began to rain and rain, then the rain turned to ice, then the ice turned to snow. There were layers of ice on the roads and almost 3 inches of snow on top of the ice. It shut the city down for over a week. There was no activity. Dallas looked like a ghost town—no schools, no work, no one out on the roads. This has never happened in the history of our city. All the interstate highways were closed coming in and out of the city until the day of the Super Bowl.

There was not one case of prostitution or sex trafficking because of this weird phenomena. This report came not only from organizations we partnered with, but also from newspaper articles.

A friend from TheCall contacted me that week with a dream that she felt was for us. In the dream she saw girls who were trapped in sex slavery. They were crying and heartbroken because of their plight. As their tears fell, Jesus caught them in His hands and they turned to blocks of ice. She asked the Lord why their tears turned to ice. He said, "It's My Just-ICE." His justice. In the form of *ice*. She told me that our ice storm was God's answer to our cry that no one would be trafficked, and Dallas would be spared from an increase in prostitution.[1]

We are here to take dominion, to ask God what can and cannot be allowed in our cities, nations, communities, and homes. All creation will respond to the priests who reign and the kings who rule. Whether it is sickness, disease, poverty, injustice, weather, sin, or saving the lost, we own the airwaves and should always be releasing God's words on earth.

Nations—Victory Over the Gates of Hell

Our commission from Jesus is to overcome the gates of hell and transform not only our families, our communities, and our regions, but *nations*. The enemy will not be able to stand against His victorious Church as we preach the gospel of the Kingdom around the world and train people to live as Jesus lived. Jesus said:

> *...on this rock I will build My church, and the gates of Hades shall not prevail against it* (Matthew 16:18).
>
> *"Go therefore and make disciples of all the nations, baptizing them in the name of the Father and of the Son and of the Holy Spirit, teaching them to observe all things that I have commanded you; and lo, I am with you always, even to the end of the age." Amen* (Matthew 28:19-20).

One of our worship leaders had been serving as a missionary in Honduras for a couple of years. She was really digging a well of revival through fasting and prayer. She laid an incredible foundation through her love and commitment to the people in Catacamas—at the time it was one of the most dangerous places in the world. She invited me to come and preach at a crusade she was hosting.

My 15-year-old son, Samuel, and I went to love on her communities. Almost every family there had been touched by the loss of a loved one to murder. They don't have running water or electricity, and their homes are made of cement blocks. I asked the Lord what He wanted me to preach, and He said,

"Teach them about how the Kingdom works through giving money and the power of their words." We had such a great time preaching the gospel of the Kingdom and seeing many set free of demonic spirits. Seeing them experience freedom as these demons came out of them was certainly intense. However, this was calm compared to what the Lord had prepared next.

On our way back toward the capital, our worship leader asked to stop by the federal prison to visit a couple of young disciples who had been falsely accused. This was a maximum security, all-male prison for murderers and rapists. I had been to prisons in the United States before, so I had presumed this experience would be similar. I presumed wrong. I imagined going in with our guitar, singing some worship songs, and talking to these guys in closed quarters. I was wrong.

As we passed through the metal detector, they took our bodyguard's gun and processed us like usual. We were led *into* the prison by the warden. I mean inside the main room where the prisoners freely roamed. No bars, no double-paned glass wall, nothing separating us from these men. It was me, my son, our bodyguard, our worship leader, and our interpreter.

The warden was taking us through the general population filled with shirtless men with teardrops tattooed under their eyes. They had obvious stab and gunshot wounds on their torsos. All of my internal alarms were going off. My son began to flank my back. Our bodyguard, who was an ex-gang member from the largest cartel in the nation, was in a full out panic. There were no guards protecting us, nor were there any guards we could see. To say that we were the main attraction is an understatement. Every eye was on us in a very aggressive way. I was praying in tongues like crazy.

We were led to an outdoor covered arena and through a door where the Catholics held chapel. I was so relieved that we were behind a door. Then they began taking chairs out into the arena. I asked why they were moving the chairs, and the warden said that we couldn't be in the chapel; we had to meet with the two boys out in the arena. I could feel my heart about to explode. I was trying to be cool, but truly I felt like I was moving in slow motion, preparing for my death. Like I was entering the gates of hell. I kept thinking to myself, *These skinny jeans were a bad idea.*

As we went out to the arena, word had circulated that we were there, so most of the prisoners had gathered in the arena. All eyes were on us. As we sat down, I made eye contact with some of the prisoners and realized that too was a bad idea. This was a large group of men, many of whom were convicted of murder and rape and probably hadn't seen a woman in months or years. And there I was in my skinny jeans with all of these men looking right at me. My heart began racing.

We had been sitting there for about ten minutes waiting as our worship leader was tuning her guitar. Then I hear the Holy Spirit say, "I want you to preach the gospel."

I laughed and said, "Oh no, that's not a good idea."

Again, He said, "I want you to preach the gospel."

So I turned to my son and said, "The Lord wants me to preach the gospel."

In shock he said, "Here?"

So I turned to my interpreter and told him the same message. His eyeballs turned to saucers. As I stood up, Samuel flanked my rear and said, "I'll kill anyone who tries to hurt you and you'll just have to raise them from the dead." So I have Samuel at my back and my interpreter at my side.

Now you have to remember that there are no guards present.

I said loudly, "Hello, I have been sent here by Jesus to tell you how much He loves you! Can you all come closer?" I'm thinking to myself, *What am I saying!?* So the men began to gather around me. I was seriously terrified. There was such a strong presence of the demonic. I mustered up all my courage and preached the gospel of the Kingdom of heaven. Then I did something that the Holy Spirit found amusing, I asked if anyone wanted to give their lives to the Lord today. Not one person came forward or raised their hands. Crickets. Not a sound.

Then I heard the Holy Spirit laughing and He said, "This is not North Dallas. Ask them if anyone needs healing in their body." *Oh right, that's a good idea.* So I asked the question, and slowly one man came forward and said he had kidney disease and was in a lot of pain. I prayed for him, the pain left, and he was immediately healed. He received Jesus and the baptism of the Holy Spirit. Then I asked him to tell the other inmates what just happened.

I then asked again, "Does anyone else need healing?" Another man stepped forward and again the power of God healed him, he gave his life to Jesus, and was baptized in the Holy Spirit. All of a sudden, the large crowd of inmates began to form a single line behind I was the man ministering to. I was amazed. Inmate after inmate was healed, saved, and baptized in fire.

Then the door to the Catholic chapel swung open and out came the Catholic inmates who were behind the closed door. Now they are watching what the Holy Spirit is doing and how these inmates are being touched by God. They saw grown, violent men crying and getting healed. Several of the Catholic guys cut in line and asked me what was happening and how they could have what I have. I told them about the power of the Holy Spirit that saves and baptizes with power. I led them through a prayer of salvation to make sure they were saved. They received Jesus as Lord and got baptized in the Holy Spirit.

Then I saw the warden and he told me I had to leave. The inmates realize what was happening and began to charge toward me to make sure they received prayer before I left. Knowing I wouldn't have time to pray for each, one on one, I shouted aloud to them that they could all have the power of God's love. I asked all who were sick to raise their hands and asked if they wanted to receive Jesus and then asked the Holy Spirit to heal them. They started yelling about fire they felt in their bodies, as the warden was dragging me out by my arm. As I was exiting the prison, several inmates were following me, touching my hand, trying to get close to me. I was amazed at the power of preaching the Kingdom of God and seeing transformation in such a short period of time. When I arrived, the prisoners saw a woman and looked at me with lust—but as I was leaving, they saw me as holy, a daughter of the King.

These men were not only in a physical prison, but a spiritual prison and bound by the prince of darkness. But the gospel of the Kingdom and the anointing of the Holy Spirit brings freedom to the captives (Luke 4:18). Their hearts were set free from the prison of darkness and filled with the light of Jesus Christ. When we follow the leading of the Holy Spirit and preach the gospel with power—even though we may feel terrified—the gates of hell will not prevail and nations will be transformed. When our words become His words, the "Grace, Grace" anointing comes upon us and every mountain becomes a plain.

The Word of God works. The Word of God is not just for story time or memorization. It is God's creative power then and now. We are called to be one with God through His Word and His love so we can create the future with Him. I am one with Christ; and as I receive His Word as a priest and use His Word as a king, I bring heaven to earth. As we become one with His Word, being fully convinced of who He is and who He is in us, we are victorious in our families, our communities, our cities and the nations.

Closing Words

I have been carrying the message of Zerubbabel's temple since He saved me with His command, "Rebuild My temple" in 1999. This has been a labor of love and a journey of discovering the revelation of God's mystery for our generation. I believe with all my heart that we are entering into our finest hour when we will see those who have become the tabernacle of God, who have come out of confusion and into the truth.

As I have shared in the prophetic chapters, God has released signs on earth and in the heavens so we can know that now is the time and now is the hour for His Melchizedek priests to function in His full governmental authority in every area of influence: family, church, government, media, arts and entertainment, business, and education.

We are living in exciting days. God has placed a prophetic Cyrus over our nation and the nations to open double doors for the priest and kings to function. The Lord has released angelic messengers saying, "The plumb line is now in the hands of Zerubbabel." He has sent prophetic messages through His prophets about Zerubbabel's temple being rebuilt. Are we listening to what the Spirit is saying to the Church in this hour and how will we respond?

Those who reign as priests and rule as kings will fulfill the mandate of Isaiah 61:4,6,7. I close this book with a declaration over you from these very verses. Receive them, meditate on them, and step into the destiny the Lord has given us.

> *And you shall rebuild the old ruins, you shall raise up the former desolations, and you shall repair the ruined cities, the desolations of many generations. You will be named priests of the Lord, they shall call you the servants of our God. You shall eat the riches of the Gentiles, and in their glory you shall boast. Instead of your shame you shall have double honor, and instead of confusion you shall rejoice in your portion. Therefore, in your land you shall possess double; everlasting joy shall be yours.*

Endnote

1. "Falling ice at Super Bowl stadium injures workers," NBCNEWS.com, February 4, 2011; http://www.nbcnews.com/id/41402775/ns/weather/t/falling-ice-super-bowl-stadium-injures-workers/#.W60Qry2ZORs, accessed July 25, 2020.

PART FOUR

PROPHETIC WORDS ABOUT ZERUBBABEL

The following are prophetic words on Zerubbabel from national and international prophetic voices:

MATT SORGER, *"Awakening: The Invasion of God Into Our Culture,"* MAY 2, 2006

While I was in Texas, covering a lot of territory, I found one ingredient was the same wherever I went. The people were hungry and desperate for a fresh move of God.

The Heart of Texas Will Be Revived—Awakening the Heart of America

The Lord communicated His heart to me in a profound way during my time in Texas. One night, as I stepped to the pulpit, I was instantly caught up into an open-eyed vision. As the Spirit caught me up, I could see the entire state of Texas. Then I saw a large heart beginning to beat stronger and stronger; it was the heart of Texas. The Holy Spirit spoke to me and said, "I am about to revive and awaken the heart of Texas. When you see the heart of Texas revived, the heart of the nation will be revived as well." In the midst of this vision I realized that Texas held a key to releasing national revival in America.

We are about to see Texas visited with a mighty move of the Holy Spirit. As the heart of the Church is revived and awakened in Texas, it will then cause an Awakening to hit the entire nation of the United States of America; turning the heart of our nation toward God.

Governmental Authority Is Being Given to Reverse the Death Culture

Dallas is a key city in Texas. There is a governmental authority God is giving to Dallas to reverse the death culture that was released over our nation in Roe v. Wade back in 1973. As the heart of Texas is revived, we will see a reversal of this death culture and the Spirit of Life released over our nation. Dallas, Texas, is a key city for prophetic decrees to be released and to see a breakthrough in the Supreme Court of America.

Three Groups Will Be Visited: Government Leaders, Spiritual Leaders, and the Remnant

As Awakening is released in our nation, not only will it revive and renew the Church, but we will also see a shift come as society begins to be radically impacted by this move of God. This anointing and outpouring will reach into many areas of society and bring great Kingdom transformation.

Haggai 1:7, 8, 14 and Haggai 2:1-9, are key Scriptures for the Awakening that is upon us. God speaks through the prophet Haggai, for the people to consider their ways and to build God's temple, so that He may be glorified. In Haggai 1:14, the Lord "stirred up" the spirit of Zerubbabel—the governor of Judah, and the high priest, Joshua, and the remnant of the people—to build the house of the Lord so that God could have a temple in which to dwell.

As the prophetic voice was released, there was a supernatural stirring that took place. In Hebrew the phrase "to stir" is *ur*, which means "to awaken, to stir up, to excite, to raise up, to arouse to action, to open one's eyes." It means "to awaken someone from sleep and rouse them to a place of action." This awakening hits three groups of people: the governor, the high priest, and the remnant. The Lord showed me that there will be three groups of people hit with this Awakening: political leaders, spiritual leaders, and the remnant in the Church.

We will see the prophetic word of the Lord invade the government arena as God opens doors for His servants to prophesy the word of the Lord to government leaders. God's Spirit will even invade the Oval Office of the White House as well as the Supreme Court. Many other political leaders will receive divine encounters as God's heart is shared with them. We will also see the hearts of many spiritual leaders across our nation and the world stirred with a fresh moving of the Holy Spirit. Their main ambition in ministry will be to build a habitation for God's glory in the earth through His Church.

We will also see the remnant of God's people arise in this hour to offer their lives in a new and deeper way as a living habitation for God's presence and glory. Kingdom pursuits will become much more important and prioritized than just living a comfortable lifestyle. People will even be willing to sacrifice, so that God's glory can have a dwelling place in the earth through their lives.

Guard Against False Comparison and Discouragement

As God's glory is outpoured and fills His house again, we must be careful not to compare what God does today with what has happened in the past. He gave me a prophetic warning not to fall into false comparison. In Haggai 2:3, the Lord saw that the people were comparing the temple God was calling them to rebuild, to what it was in its former glory in Solomon's day. Haggai 2:3 (NKJV) says, *"In comparison with it, is this not in your eyes as nothing?"* They remembered how glorious Solomon's temple was; how the cloud had filled the temple so that the priests could no longer continue ministering (2 Chronicles 5:14). An internal enemy of discouragement through false comparison was trying to hinder them from building God's temple.

As God calls us to build a habitation for His glory, we must be careful not to put God or how He moves into a "revival box." God may show up in a way that is very different from our preconceived ideas. We must be careful not to fall into a false comparison—even with past moves of God—and allow God to release His greater glory in the way He wants to do it. We must stay open and sensitive to the Holy Spirit so we don't miss Him when He comes.

Greater Glory and Supernatural Provision

Haggai prophesies in Haggai 2:4-9, *"'Yet now be strong... and work; for I am with you. ...Once more...I will shake heaven and earth, the sea and dry land; and I will shake all nations, and they shall come to the Desire of All Nations, and I will fill this temple with glory.... The silver is Mine, and the gold is Mine.... The glory of this latter temple shall be greater than the former.... And in this place I will give peace,' says the Lord of hosts."*

God's promise is that no matter what the temple looks like on the outside, the glory shall be greater on the inside! He also throws in there a promise for continual divine provision to get the job done. God reaffirms that all the gold and silver are His; He owns it all. We will see a great supernatural provision for the Church to build God's Kingdom on earth; building a place for His greater glory to dwell.

God Will Invade Our Society, in Politics and Media

There is a greater glory upon us. Awakening is about to hit America and the nations on many levels including both spiritual and political. As political leaders catch the heart of God, they will begin to rally causes that are on God's heart. This is where we will begin to see the walls broken down once again between church and state. Not only will the Church be set on fire, but society will be impacted through righteous political leaders. We will also see an invasion of God into the media. Jesus is about to be glorified in Hollywood and through the media, both secular and Christian. New networks will be formed that will glorify God. Churches must be prepared to take the airwaves for God, as a new wave of media outreach and anointing is upon us.

This next Awakening will shake the Church and bring a great transformation in our culture and society as the Holy Spirit empowers us to reach the world with His supernatural grace and power.

RICK PINO, *"Angel of Awakening,"* OCTOBER 2006

Rick Pino had an angelic visitation: The angel said, "I am the angel of Zechariah 4. It is time to awaken." A word about Angel of Awakening from Rick:

In late October 2006 I was visited by the angel of Zechariah chapter 4. In this encounter, the Lord used this messenger to speak to me about how He was going to be releasing this mighty angel to blow the trumpet of awakening in the earth the following year. The Angel of Awakening is part of that emerging sound of awakening! A sound of bones rattling in the desert! This studio project is a compilation of songs that I have received from the Lord, and songs that the Lord poured out spontaneously in the sessions. (http://rickpino.com/store/angel-of-awakening)

STEVEN L. SHELLEY, *"Angels with assignment are preparing us to receive perhaps the most astounding revelation of all time—from the open book,"* JULY 2008

Before leaving home in Salem, Alabama, the morning of July 28, 2008, I had prayed in frustration, asking the Lord to help me recapture the dream that I had experienced during the previous night. I remembered that an angel had walked into our bedroom and over to my side of the bed. He had spoken several things to me; and as he was finishing, I was awakened by our four-year-old daughter, Olivia, crying out in the night, "Daddy, that door is open, should I go through it?"

I got out of bed and walked to the doorway of her room. She was sleeping soundly. As I walked back to bed, I suddenly realized that I could not remember a single thing the angel had said to me. It was as though it had been erased from my memory.

The next morning I was scheduled to fly to Canada for a conference with Paul Keith Davis and Neville Johnson. With a stopover in Salt Lake City, I was to meet up with Paul Keith before completing our journey. I finally spotted him, and as I approached him he greeted me with, "Steven, what happened to you last night?" I must have looked shocked because he then explained that around 3 a.m. he woke up with his wife, Wanda, standing over him, asking him the same question!

Earlier that night, Wanda had experienced a supernatural encounter. She was shown that a message of some sort was being given at that very moment to both Paul Keith and me. It was embarrassing for me to have to tell Paul Keith that even though I knew I had been visited by an angel in a dream, I could not remember anything that had been spoken to me. He agreed to help me pray that the message would not be lost.

Late that night I finally settled into my hotel room in Red Deer, Alberta, Canada. In desperation, I called out to the Lord to restore what I felt the enemy had stolen from my mind. I randomly opened my Bible and used it as a pillow and I lay on the floor and buried my face into its open pages. I was so very disappointed in myself for letting this slip, and repented in case there was anything that I had done that had caused it to be lost. I felt like a poor steward of what the Lord was saying to us.

After much weeping I raised my head and my eyes fell on the open pages of my Bible. It was opened to *Daniel chapter 2*, where the king had forgotten a dream and was asking for Daniel to tell him both the dream and the interpretation of it. I smiled inside at God's perfect timing. I was encouraged and drifted off to sleep, knowing that the Lord would restore to me the revelation that had slipped from my memory.

God didn't waste any time. I began dreaming that I was back in my bedroom in Alabama. I was somehow conscious enough to wonder in excitement if this would be the lost dream. I soon recognized the angel that I had seen the night before and determined to listen carefully to what he had to say. The dream progressed as he walked over to my side of the bed.

The Message

He said, "The plumb line is NOW in the hand of Zerubbabel."

> *For who has despised the day of small things? For these seven rejoice to see the plumb line in the hand of Zerubbabel. They are the eyes of the Lord, which scan to and fro throughout the whole earth* (Zechariah 4:10).

A "plumb line" is a simple but accurate ancient tool that is used to determine whether or not something is perfectly vertical or upright. It consists of a line and a weight of some sort. Initially a stone was used, but in later times the weight was more commonly made of lead.

I knew that in the context of this experience this plumb line spoke of a word or message from the Lord that was being released in our day that would measure, once and for all, the "uprightness" of the Bride. The very definition of the word *righteousness* is "uprightness."

> *Thus He showed me: Behold, the Lord stood on a wall made with a plumb line, with a plumb line in His hand. And the Lord said to me, "Amos, what do you see?" And I said, "A plumb line." Then the Lord said: "Behold, I am setting a plumb line in the midst of My people Israel; I will not pass by them anymore"* (Amos 7:7-8).

We have, in recent times, been guilty perhaps of leaning too far to the left or too far to the right. I knew that the angel was saying that it was time to examine how we were standing and to make the necessary adjustments immediately. We can only make these important changes by examining our lives according to the clear plumb line message of the Kingdom being released by God in the earth NOW. In addition, we must cooperate fully with the double grace (see Zechariah 4:7) that is being extended to the Bride in this season.

Interestingly, Zerubbabel is the one who led the first band of Jews back to Jerusalem from Babylonian captivity. This exodus took place in the first year of Cyrus, the king of Persia. We also learn that Zerubbabel laid the foundation for the second temple.

> *The hands of Zerubbabel have laid the foundation of this house; his hands shall also finish it; and thou shalt know that the LORD of hosts hath sent me unto you* (Zechariah 4:9 KJV).

It becomes clear that as Zerubbabel was a builder of the natural temple, these same Scriptures prophesy of the building of a spiritual temple. Zerubbabel is a type of the Master Builder, who is shaping and molding His people into a temple in which He can dwell with all His fullness. Zerubbabel's perseverance in the completion of the earthly temple is a prophetic sign to us that the Lord Jesus will also prevail in finishing the spiritual temple that He is building in and through us.

> *And I am convinced and sure of this very thing, that He Who began a good work in you will continue until the day of Jesus Christ [right up to the time of His return], developing [that good work] and perfecting and bringing it to full completion in you* (Philippians 1:6 Amplified Bible, Classic Edition).

I then asked the angel, "Who are you?"

"I am one of those who has been sent to prepare a people to receive the open book and to eat it!" he answered boldly.

I believe that this was the Lord speaking clearly of a people in this hour, who were chosen before the foundation of the world, to discover hidden treasures that have been reserved in darkness. These hidden treasures are truths that were sealed and not available to the Body of Christ for many centuries—until NOW.

> *And I will give thee the treasures of darkness, and hidden riches of secret places, that thou mayest know that I, the LORD, which call thee by thy name, am the God of Israel* (Isaiah 45:3 KJV).

Taste and See

Perhaps some wonder why these mysteries were hidden for so long. The answer is twofold. First, these truths were reserved until this generation because we have now crossed that threshold into the end of days to which these truths are at long last relevant. Second, there were things concealed in this open book which, because of their spiritual implications, made it imperative that they be hidden from our enemy. Just think what damage might have been done had they fallen into satan's hands at the wrong time or ahead of God's great times and seasons.

Satan is constantly trying to cause things to engage earlier than their appointed time. Prayer warriors are often being arrested to pray against this plot of the enemy to preempt the timing of the Lord. Because of this strategy of the enemy, it requires that we as a body of believers walk even more sensitively and in total agreement with the purposes and seasons of the Lord (see 1 Chronicles 12:32).

It is part of the overcomer's calling to receive this openbook revelation and to eat it. We read in Revelation 10:9-11 that

John was told to eat it up. He was also warned that it would be sweet in his mouth, reminding us of the sweetness of true revelation. John was further warned that the book would be bitter in his belly. This speaks of the effect that these revelations will have inside the believer. As these truths are made real to us we will not be able to keep them inside; they are not for us only but must come out of us again as we prophesy these end-time truths to many peoples and nations and tongues and kings.

It is refreshing for us to know that in these troubled and uncertain times when we often feel overwhelmed and insufficient for the task of harvest, that God is releasing angels who find and mark those who hunger for deeper truths. These angels will then help to prepare us to open our hearts for Kingdom mysteries. Additionally, they will release God's grace over us to step aside, when necessary, from our own opinions and interpretations of the Word.

Angelic Convergence

A few weeks ago we were gathered once again in Red Deer for the annual "Rivers of God's Love" conference. Again God chose to speak to me in a dream. I was given a pair of very old binoculars and then instructed to look through them. As I placed them before my eyes, I saw two groups of angels coming in, one from the east and one from the west. They were converging in the middle and teaming up in pairs. I then saw them being dispatched to various places throughout the world. I then took the binoculars away from my eyes and realized that I could no longer see the angels.

"What was I seeing?" I asked.

The messenger replied, "This day begins a new cooperation in the angelic realm. Two classes of angels who each have distinct commissions are now being joined together in full cooperation for a season of ministry."

I found this so fascinating that once again I placed the old binoculars up to my eyes and carefully examined the scene before me.

The angels coming in from the west looked almost identical in every way. Their robes matched in every detail down to the trimmings. They seemed oddly familiar to me. I suddenly realized that the one who had come to me in Alabama was one of these. I could only surmise that these were the angels who were being sent to prepare a people to receive and to eat the open book!

I then asked the messenger who had given me the binoculars, "Who are these other angels coming in from the east?" I had noticed that they were also quite similar to each other, but I observed that there were variations in the belts that they wore.

"These are angels that gather," I was told. Although I was very familiar with Paul Keith's encounter with them, this was my first time seeing them.

He then restated to me what I had concluded on my own: *"There will now be a divine cooperation between the angels that gather and the angels that are sent to prepare a people to receive and eat the open book."*

We are living in incredibly exciting days. Angels are being dispatched to help prepare us to receive, eat, and digest perhaps the most astounding revelation of all time—the revelation of the open book! We may not yet have the full understanding of what this angelic cooperation will look like, but I am convinced that it certainly means that help is on the way. More than ever, humility is the order of the day. Declare with your mouth that you are *hungry* and willing to do whatever it takes to be a vital part of what God has in store.

For further understanding of what the revelation of the "open book" is about, read Daniel 12:1-4, Revelation chapters 5, 6, and 10. (http://www.elijahlist.com/words/display _word/8046)

JEFF AND JAN JANSEN, *"Synchronizing Heaven and Earth— the Plumb Line in the Hand of Zerubbabel,"* JUNE 17, 2009.

The Plumb Line for the New Temple—A Visitation

In a visitation the Lord appeared to me and said, "The plumb line is falling," and I saw a plumb line fall into place. Webster's describes a plumb line as a cord that has weight, which is used to find "verticality"—whether or not a wall is perfectly vertical.

Zechariah 4:10 says that men will *"rejoice when they see the plumb line in the hand of Zerubbabel,"* and verse 7 says that *"he shall bring forth the finishing gable stone* [or capstone] *[of the new temple] with loud shoutings of the people, crying, Grace, grace to it!"* (Amplified Bible, Classic Edition).

Paul wrote to the church in Ephesians telling them that we are the temple of God. He said:

> *You are built upon the foundation of the apostles and prophets with Christ Jesus Himself the chief Cornerstone. In Him the whole structure is joined (bound, welded) together harmoniously, and it continues to rise (grow, increase) into a holy temple in the Lord [a sanctuary dedicated, consecrated, and sacred to the presence of the Lord]. In Him [and in fellowship with one another] you yourselves also are being built up [into this structure] with the rest, to form a fixed abode (dwelling place) of God in (by, through) the Spirit* (Ephesians 2:20-22 AMPC).

Peter writes:

> *[Come] and, like living stones, be yourselves built [into] a spiritual house, for a holy (dedicated, consecrated) priesthood, to offer up [those] spiritual sacrifices[that are] acceptable and pleasing to God through Jesus Christ* (1 Peter 2:5 AMPC).

We are the new temple! This new temple is coming forth with shouts of "Grace, grace!" Shout, "Grace" as the mountains of human obstacles that have resisted the anointing and the power of the Kingdom begin to crumble and fade from view! God is anointing a generation to move in the knowledge of the glory of the Lord as the waters cover the sea (see Habakkuk 2:14). The Lord will display this new temple, this spiritual house in the earth, as a people anointed with the kingly-priestly anointing found in Zechariah 4. They will flow with the ceaseless supply of the golden oil of the Holy Spirit and will function with unlimited anointing.

The plumb line was in the hand of Zerubbabel who was king of Judah. The kingly anointing, mixed with the high praises of Judah, will cause the Holy Spirit to explode in massive revival fires throughout the world resulting in a clash of the kingdoms! *God's people will rise from the darkness and shine so brightly with His power and glory that the nations will run to the house of God to see it (see Isaiah 60)!*

This new temple is not one built with brick and mortar, but is the Spirit-filled Church *(ecclesia:* called-out ones) of the living God. We are His temple! He lives in us and His Kingdom is in us!

Zechariah 4:6 says, *"'Not by might nor by power, but by My Spirit,' says the LORD of hosts."* This plumb line will fall as a result of God bringing the capstone for the new temple which is just and true. It's not a human thing, it's a God thing. It's not by might nor by power, nor by the strong arm of the flesh nor by the works of any man—it's by "My Spirit," says the Lord! God is building an end-time temple in accordance with the word of Haggai the prophet:

> *"...and I will shake all the nations, and they shall come to the Desire of All Nations, and I will fill this temple with glory,"* says the LORD of hosts. *"The silver is Mine, and the gold is Mine,"* says the LORD of hosts. *"The glory of this latter temple* [you and me] *shall be greater than the former..."* (Haggai 2:7-9).

This plumb line that sets the capstone of the latter-day temple will be greater and more beautiful and majestic than the glory of Solomon's temple. All the kings of the earth and even the Queen of Sheba came to marvel at the sight of Solomon's temple and to hear his profound wisdom. But the nations will stream into the house of God to see the glory of His splendor in the temple of the Lord manifested in and through His people—the "Perusia"—the ever-increasing presence of God and indwelling glory of God.

The Church will be greater in splendor, wisdom, and glory than even Solomon's temple! However, in order for this to happen, there must first be a reestablishing of balance in His Body according to the fallen plumb line set in eternity.

A Time of Choosing Sides

The Lord spoke to Jan about His glory and said that with this plumb line, everyone will have to choose which side they are on. Those who choose His glory will receive it in a greater measure than they ever imagined! I saw a joyous celebration taking place with spectacular manifestations of the glory of God! Those who chose God would ascend to higher and higher levels in glory and into intimacy with the Father, Son, and Holy Spirit—they would be qualified to go to the next level.

She also saw many who resisted His glory. They missed out on this glorious level of God's presence and were drawn away into unbelief—into increased legalism and a religious spirit began to dominate those who were once full of faith and belief.

Jesus Christ didn't come preaching a religion of word alone, but rather He came preaching the Gospel of the Kingdom with evidence. Jesus' biggest problem was with the unbelieving and religious people, not the broken. Unbelief cuts us off from the promises He is speaking—it keeps us from entering His rest (see Hebrews 3:12–4:16).

Standing on the Side of the Supernatural

The Lord said this was a "NOW" word and we must ask ourselves, "What do we believe about supernatural encounters and experiences? What do we believe about the Kingdom of God and the angelic realm?" God is moving like never before in the earth. It's time to believe, to stand, and to speak in faith. Let's stand on the right side of the plumb line—the right side of the issue. As we do, the Lord will fill us with revelation insight and power as we shine as bright lights that will change our world. God will back us up with all of the economics and provisions of heaven. (http://www.elijahlist.com/words/display_word/7744)

ABOUT THE AUTHOR

Tracy Eckert is executive pastor and cofounder of Storehouse, a house of prayer and church committed to establishing worship and prayer in Dallas, Texas, and training leaders as kings and priests to access heaven and transform the earth. She is anointed to preach the gospel, prophesy to cities and nations, heal the sick and brokenhearted. Tracy and her husband, John, have seven children and twelve grandchildren.

Contact Information
Website: www.tracyeckert.com
Twitter: @tracyeckert
Instagram: @tracyeckert
Facebook: @tracy.eckert.10

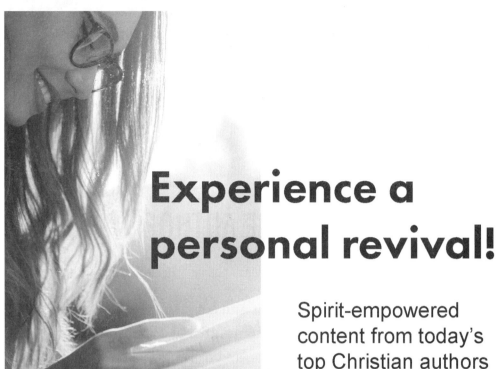